PSYCHOLOGICAL SPIRITUALITY

PSYCHOLOGICAL
SPIRITUALITY

Keith Hill

attar books

First edition published in 2020 by Attar Books
Auckland, New Zealand

Paperback ISBN 978-0-9951333-0-3
Hardcover ISBN 978-0-9951333-2-7
Ebook ISBN 978-0-9951333-1-0

Cover image by Lightspring/Shutterstock

Attar Books is a New Zealand publisher which focuses on work that explores today's spiritual experiences, culture, concepts and practices. For more information visit our website:

www.attarbooks.com

CONTENTS

PREFACE

F OR OVER TEN YEARS I HAVE BEEN CHANNELLING MATERIAL THAT
deals with the implications of being human. I have received this material from non-embodied identities who say they are the same as us, that they
have previously lived as human beings but have moved beyond incarnation
and now exist in a non-physical domain.

Historically, humanity has characterised this non-physical domain as
spiritual, and has assumed our soul goes there after our body dies. For that
reason it is popularly known as the afterlife. However, the problem with
"the afterlife" is we know practically nothing about it. And most of what we
do know is contained in ancient religious narratives that reference gods, angels, demons, and saved and condemned souls, each of whom occupy zones
that Christianity identifies as heaven, hell and purgatory, and Tibetan Bud-
dhism as bardos. Today our intellectual preference is for direct evidence,
so ancient religious narratives—which are vague, at best, and are often em-
bellished to reflect dogmatic positions—do not offer sufficiently convincing
details regarding how the afterlife is constituted, who resides there, and how
they occupy themselves—assuming the identities I interact with are not the
only ones living there, and that the religious categories of gods, angels and
demons don't encompass all the varieties of non-physical beings.

This nebulous cognisance of the afterlife has another major weakness.
The non-embodied identities I channel maintain that where they exist
cannot be called the afterlife because they inhabited that zone both before
and after they incarnated into human bodies. Moreover, they assert they

also occupied it while incarnated—this fascinating possibility is discussed in *Where Do I Go When I Meditate?*, in a chapter titled "Is All of Me Here?"). They additionally claim that their embodiment in human form has been just one phase in their ongoing efforts to develop as spiritual identities, and that the non-physical domain they currently occupy is actually their normal zone of residence. All this means our characterisation of the spiritual domain as "the afterlife" is incorrect.

Where this claim gains added significance is that if the channelled identities really are spiritual beings who have completed their cycles of incarnation, and if we are the same spiritual species as them, then their nature and normal zone of residence is also ours. Supposedly, then, we are non-physical beings, our natural state is non-embodiment, and our natural home is in a non-physical zone.

Of course, I have no way of proving any of this. To acknowledge this as the case I have used the qualifiers "claim", "assert" and "supposedly", leaving space for readers to decide for themselves how much of this material they will accept. In mitigation, I add that the channelled identities have always seemed trustworthy to me. They have never been coercive, and have always answered my questions in a generous, rational, grounded and thorough manner. Neither have they ever said anything or acted in any way that triggered doubts in me. In addition, I have occasionally interacted with them in other situations, besides channelling their thoughts—for example, while meditating, via visions, in dreams, and even through thoughts they projected into my mind during the course of everyday living. None of these interactions has led me to suspect they are not who they say they are. They have always come across as experienced, insightful, respectful and compassionate.

From a sceptical viewpoint, all this may suggest I am trapped inside a self-justifying bubble, which I am incapable of seeing out of. I offer this book, and the other channelled books I have helped produce to date, in response. Ultimately, it is for each reader to weigh the channelled words against their own knowledge and experience and decide on their validity for themselves. The guides ("guides" is my preferred designation of them) also say they are happy to interact directly with those who wish to do so, albeit reserving the right to decide who they respond to.

With that clarified, I will make one more comment on this material. If I was asked to identify a single theme that predominates through everything I have channelled to date, that theme is reincarnation. The main implicaton of reincarnation is that we are not just spiritual identities who incarnate in human bodies, we do so repeatedly, until we have extracted all we can from the experience. Only then do we move on to what comes next. According to the guides, this process takes an average of one thousand incarnations.

If this is the case, being human involves a serious commitment! It also means that our traditional one-life view of human existence is inadequate. Trying to make sense of the often startling differences between individuals' temperaments, capabilities, morality, skills, coping abilities, ability to antici-pate, and plain understanding of what is going on, while assuming we only live once, can never succeed. We need much wider conceptual frameworks, which take into account that every one of us is progressing through an ex-tended series of lifetimes. The multi-life perspective is that we each have our individual priorities and experientially-derived knowledge, as a result of which we possess very different perspectives, skill-sets, and levels of under-standing. In addition, we are all at different phases in an individual, unique journey that lasts for approximately one thousand lives.

Psychological Spirituality focuses on human psychology as it functions within this multi-life framework. The greatest difficulties we face, along with the psychological strengths and weaknesses that loom largest in our life, have their roots in prior life experience. This makes our individual psychological make-up, as it exists in this life, the tip of an iceberg that has been formed by previous experiences, choices and reactions. It also means that the bulk of who we are remains hidden from our immediate perception. It is only by adopting a multi-life perspective that we can get to the heart of who we are and what is driving us in this life.

Psychological Spirituality is needed because we currently understand very little about the impact of repeated incarnation. This book adds signifi-cantly to our appreciation of how human psychology is shaped by reincarna-tion. I have personally found the information revelatory. My initial spiritual training was in G.I. Gurdjieff's Fourth Way Teaching, to which I was in-troduced in a New Zealand group led by a Naqshbandi shaykh, Abdullah

Dougan. The group's emphasis was on identifying psychological traits in order to work on them, developing traits that are advantageous, and either transforming or eliminating those that are not. This psychological work is necessary both to develop our potential as human beings and to purify ourselves inwardly to become capable of having subtle spiritual insights. More recently, I have been introduced to the channelled Michael Teachings, which expands Gurdjieff's ideas by adding contemporary self-transformational ideas and practices, and especially by introducing a multi-life framework to our understanding of being human. This book contributes to that move. As such, it draws on the Gurdjieff and Michael Teachings, and adds new complementary material.

I consider *Psychological Spirituality* provides a singular and helpful view of how reincarnation helps shape our identity and growth. I hope therapists, as well as seekers, find its conceptual tools useful for understanding human psychospiritual development within a multi-life framework. I now hand the keyboard over to the guides.

Keith Hill
March 2020, Kimihia, New Zealand

FROM THE GUIDES

We appreciate our scribe's concern to clarify what has been undertaken in the series of books we have collectively collaborated on to date, and intend to keep producing into the foreseeable future. We reiterate that his understanding of what is taking place in these exchanges is correct. We, that is, those who are dictating these words, are the same as you. The difference between us is that we have experienced and completed what you, the readers of this text, are currently working through. This doesn't make us better or superior to you. However, it could be said we are more experienced, because we have built on our successes and learned from our mistakes, and so have extracted a little of what may be termed *wisdom* from the experience of being immersed in the human domain. In this sense, we could be described as your older siblings. That the individual who is channelling this text has denoted us "guides", while we consonantly denote him "scribe", is merely convenient labelling, of use in a human social context. We reiterate, we are the same as our scribe, and as you, our readers, just being a little further along in our development. It is on this basis, and particularly in the light of having ourselves been through what you are now experiencing, that we are offering what we intend to be useful advice.

Of course, what readers do with what we are offering is up to them. In fact, it is not necessary to do anything with it at all. Sometimes knowledge itself is sufficient, given it is then lodged within your mind and so is available to be accessed when needed. However, our intent is to share what, from the everyday human perspective, provides perhaps startlingly new perspectives on human incarnation in order for readers to use that information to positively influence their current life.

Knowledge leads to freedom. This is a long-standing adage which we readily endorse. Knowing how an engine runs helps an engineer diagnose why the engine is not running optimally, then fix it. Without knowledge of the engine there is no way to diagnose and correct the malfunction. The same applies to the human psyche. Everyone's psyche has traits that limit their functioning. Those negative traits narrow your perception of your life situation, which is that you are a spiritual identity who has incarnated in a human body. Knowing this is the first step to freedom—because in your essential nature you are free, and to a degree inconceivable to those whose perception is confined to looking out through the narrow chinks of the human mind and its body's five senses.

Self-transformation is the key to becoming freer while inhabiting a human body. The knowledge we are offering is intended to provide ideas and practices that can be applied practically so you may achieve greater freedom within your psyche. One of the key changes of perspectives that all incarnated human beings need to achieve before they are able to complete their cycle of incarnations is to appreciate that their innate nature is spiritual, and to understand this not just theoretically but directly, in relation to their personal trajectory through the human domain. This involves accessing what, later in the book, we identify as their accumulated human identity.

Delving into the fullness of what you are is a step-by-step process. It begins with receiving knowledge regarding your innate nature, by whatever means and in whatever form. We make this conditional statement because no one delivery format, no one sequence of content, can offer a complete description of the human situation. Neither does any transmission, whether in religious or any other form, offer a full programme for self-transformation. Self-transformation operates on too many levels, and incorporates too many subtleties, to be captured in any text. Additionally, no set of information, again whether it is religiously encoded or presented in another form, can ever be equally meaningful to everyone, given differences in personal experience, perception and inclination. This means that any knowledge provided to the incarnated is necessarily provisional. No knowledge set is, or can be, complete in itself. Yet even partial information can still be useful and so be worth sharing, if it is done on the basis of what is useful now, and at a level those it is offered to can make sense of and use. Such an awareness is behind everything we are sharing through our scribe. The various books and communications we have initiated have slightly different purposes, and are offered to readers who possess differing levels of experience and understanding. But unifying all our channelled material is a desire to share a point-of-view that, from your perspective, likely appears as somewhat elevated and expansive, and to express it in terms that may be of use to those who read it.

Within this intent, we can broadly state that the *Channelled Q+A Series* of books offers an introductory view of the human situation (although it also explores some ideas and practices relevant to more experienced individuals), while the *Channelled Spirituality Series* focuses on the impact serial incarnation has on how a life is lived, and on how that life may be understood more deeply and consequently lived more effectively. Specifically, this book adds to the material presented in the first two books in the *Channelled Spirituality Series*. *Experimental Spirituality* puts forward in general terms the purpose of human existence and the issues involved in being a spirit that repeatedly incarnates in a human body. It also introduces the concept of the five-layered self as a means to understand human psychospiritual make-up. *Practical Spirituality* examines the preconditions that apply when planning a life and how blockages and limiting psychological factors impede the realisation of an individual's life plan.

The purpose of *Psychological Spirituality* is to extend our examination of the human psychospiritual make-up utilising the paired concepts of true personality and false personality. Contrasting these two psychological aspects will cast light on why some lives achieve satisfactory conclusions and others conclude unsatisfactorily. Note, however, that in the sense intended here, *satisfactory* and *unsatisfactory* have nothing to do with whether a life was spent happily or unhappily, was easy or complex, or resulted in much or apparently little being achieved.

In our terms, *satisfactory* has entirely to do with achieving life goals and realising a significant percentage of the life plan—because, in fact, that life plan may have involved dealing with the consequences of unhappiness and learning to be strong through it, or with exploring complex and difficult situations or relationships, or in achieving what appears to have been only a little, yet achieving that little fully and in great depth. This is in contrast to superficially achieving much but actually going into situations half-heartedly and ending up poorly working through chosen tasks. On the spiritual level, as on the human everyday level, superficial evaluations can deceive.

Human psychology is complicated. It contains many locks. Our intention is to provide you, throughout this series of five books, with the keys you require to open those locks. Of course, not everyone wants this. The reason is not difficult to discern. The human psyche is a Pandora's Box. Opening it releases undesired memories of all kinds of distasteful childhood incidents, along with nasty feelings and horrible thoughts, the reperception of which makes life miserable. Then there are the negativities in the psyche's basement, at the very bottom of Pandora's Box. Opening the door to the basement releases ghouls that shake perceptions, stir up anxieties, and destabilise even the most apparently stable life. Accordingly, it is understandable that very few people wish to open the Pandora's Box of their psyche: they don't want to deal with issues they have worked so hard to forget.

The situation is the same for spiritual seekers who wish to bathe in the heavenly glades of their spirit. They certainly don't want to wade waist-deep in the fires of hell. Yet hell must be traversed. Why? Because otherwise individuals continue to carry unresolved trauma, negative emotions and attitudes, and self-limiting behaviours that, however well buried, and however long they remain hidden, will eventually flare up and burn to cinders the delightful glade in which they wish to stroll. And, of course, by "hell" and "flames" we do not refer to nasty places the unwary may enter, although they certainly do exist. Rather, we refer to the negative aspects of the human psychospiritual make-up. Such negative aspects are psychospiritual because they are not limited to this life. Rather, they are carried from life to life. And if they are not addressed they continue to impact negatively life after life.

We have grouped these negative and self-limiting emotions, attitudes, traits and behaviours under the rubric of false personality. In one sense this is an arbitrary demarcation, because no one actually possesses a false personality. What human beings possess is a collection of psychological materials, so to speak, that collectively shape their everyday identity. Much of this material is conditioned during childhood. Some of it is chosen prior to incarnation. Some of it takes the form of negative traits attached to the essence self. And some of it is brought into this life via deep essence.

To call this mass of psychological traits false is not technically correct, because it is present to provide obstacles the individual has chosen to deal with in this life for the purpose of learning how to better negotiate the difficult task of living as a spirit within a human body. So what we are calling false personality may equally, and definitely more accurately, be termed obstacle personality. Just as validly, what we are calling true personality, being the collection of positive traits centred on the essence self and its moving, emotional and intellectual capacities, may more properly be termed the seeding personality. This is because these positive qualities grow as a result of self-transformation and contribute to the blooming of the evolving spirit.

This metaphor may be extended by comparing an individual's growth to that of a grapevine. On the whole, vines develop grapes with the most intense flavours when they are in stony and well-drained soils. The principle is that when vines have to fight the environment for nutrition they develop greater flavour. The more they fight, the better the quality of the grapes. Similarly, it can be said that the more obstacles an individual spirit addresses and overcomes in its struggles to experience, learn and grow, the deeper the lessons it draws from its experiences, and the correspondingly greater its eventual levels of love, knowledge and wisdom. In this way obstacles and what is learned as they are worked through flavour the evolving spirit. To describe this transformation in developmental terms, positively overcoming obstacles, without impinging on others in the process, is a sign of increasing maturity. And the more complex and demanding the obstacle, the greater the resulting maturity.

It must be noted that using the terms false personality and true personality as collective descriptions of negative and positive collections of psychological traits provides only a partial description of human psychology. The term *false* ignores what is useful in the supposedly false, and downplays the significance of obstacles for assisting in the development of positive traits and facilitating human maturity.

Nonetheless, the opposition of false personality to true personality does remain a useful piece of shorthand, because this opposition encapsulates another psychological truth about human incarnation—that a significant part of each individual's psychology constantly and unwaveringly functions to distract human beings from fulfilling the most important reason they were born, that reason being to enter the situations, meet the people, and fulfil the tasks that together constitute the activities of their life plan. Insofar as false personality fills individuals' everyday awareness with desires, feelings and thoughts that distract those individuals to the degree that they don't complete life tasks or fulfil their life plan, it may be said it "plays the individual false".

Of course, the most significant aspects of the various psychological components that constitute false personality were actually selected prior to incarnation expressly to form an obstacle, and so they have a valid place within the individual's make-up. Yet this does not lessen the fact that false personality leads individuals to be false to their own deepest self and its desires and plans.

What causes individuals to be false to their deepest desires and plans? Fear. Fear is the central emotion around which all the behaviours and traits of false personality are arrayed. So opening the Pandora's Box of the human psyche involves addressing and working on the fears that underpin all negativities. Remove the fears and negativities lose their power to "play you false". This book identifies the principle types of fears and describes how they shape the false personality's chief feature. The qualities of true personality are then explored in relation to the essence self, along with how false personality impinges on the essence self. Our overall aim is to outline a process by which inner obstacles may be overcome and false transformed into true.

As with the previous two books in this series, this is a channelled text emanating from the spiritual realm, offered to those who wish to understand their situation on Earth and who are striving to realise as much of their life plan as motivation, opportunity and sustained effort facilitates.

We wish you well in your search for self-knowledge. May these words sprinkle a little extra sustenance on your identity in this incarnation, trickle down to your roots as they draw life lessons from the gravel in your life, and feed the fruits of your personal wisdom!

PART ONE

THE NATURE OF
FALSE PERSONALITY

CHAPTER 1

Fear and its Manifestations

SIGNIFICANT SIMILARITY MAY BE OBSERVED BETWEEN HUMAN psychological make-up and spiritual identity. Just as some individual's psychological make-up is very layered and complex and for others it is simple and straightforward, so some spiritual identities are layered and others are not. Some human beings are naturally open and others are closed, with a range of variations between. On the spiritual level some identities are open and others are comparatively closed, again with a range between.

Of course, there is no one-to-one correlation between human embodied identity and spiritual non-embodied identity. One reason for this is that the constrictions placed on spiritual identity when it is embodied is that it forgets its true reality and is limited by both its body's physical sensory system and the feeling and thinking capacities of that body's nervous system and its biological brain. There is no equivalent restriction on identity at the spiritual level. Nonetheless, it could be said that the non-embodied spiritual identity *is* constricted to the range of experiences it has undergone and the life lessons it has drawn from those experiences. This larger sense of constriction is certainly reflected down into the human sub-identity that an ongoing spiritual identity adopts in any life. It is in this sense that any human sub-identity reflects the intrinsic nature and the evolved, or unevolved, state of the spirit at its core.

As a spiritual identity enters a body and "rides" it for the duration of a lifetime, its overall task is to learn to function in a knowing and loving manner. In order to achieve this it has to learn to "steer" the body it inhabits.

19

It takes a considerable number of lifetimes to learn how to do so. Why are many lives needed? Because the human being is a complex vehicle. As we have discussed in detail in the two previous books, everyday human identity comprises the interplay of genetically inherited physical qualities, innumerable socially passed on and conditioned factors, and the varied skills of the essence self's moving, emotional and intellectual capacities. All kinds of biological and social forces play into individual human beings, pushing them this way and that. These forces are at times so powerful that the individual can't control them and the life journey goes off the tracks. It may take several lifetimes of correcting before the spirit can get back on the rails and continue pursuing the goals it has set itself prior to instituting the series of incarnations that have been derailed. Chief among these numerous derailing forces is fear.

OLD BRAIN AND SPIRITUALLY SOURCED FEARS

In Chapter Five of *Experimental Spirituality* we introduced the idea that fear has two primary sources. We recommend readers review that chapter before continuing here, but will briefly summarise its conclusions.

The first source of human fear is the animal fear embedded in the old brain, also known as the reptilian brain, which gives rise to the survival behaviours of fight or flight. The second source of fear is the spiritual level fear a spirit feels when it arrives in a new environment and can't control either the body into which it has been born or the environment in which it now exists. These two levels of fear—one animal, the other spiritual—reinforce one another and together generate a powerful force that focuses an individual's awareness on its own self that functions to ensure its continued preservation.

Initially, when ancient humanity lived as hunter-gatherers in small family-centred tribes, the instinctive mechanism of fight or flight was necessary to keep individuals alive on the basic animal level. This same biological survival mechanism is of course shared with all other animal species. However, over the millennia, as later generations of humanity moved out of the foraging and hunter-gatherer lifestyle, domesticated animals and plants, and built the first towns, human beings began living together en masse and human civilization became correspondingly more complex. Social interactions reflected this new complexity and human behaviour correspondingly became more intricate.

With safety in numbers, human beings partially domesticated the wild world, holding natural threats at bay. The instinctive fear generated by the old brain then became socialized into forms of behaviour that were more useful for surviving in social groups and relationships. Of course, primal old brain fear still came out occasionally, when the veneer of civilization was ripped off and drunkenness, violence, desperation, or warring led some to beat, rape, mutilate or murder others. But this destructive behaviour was not conducive to the long-term propagation of the species. So over time the openly destructive aspects of humanity's primal fear was progressively tamed, and eventually instinctive biological fear was socialized into acceptable behaviours. Naturally, because human beings still possess the ancient reptilian old brain, instinctive fear has never gone away. Instead, its manifestations have become buried deeper and deeper within the human psyche.

One of the most significant ways that buried fear manifests in human behaviour is in humanity's fear of the stranger, fear of what is different, fear of anything or anyone that is other than themselves. The vast majority of these kinds of fear involves projecting uncontrolled, usually unperceived, buried old brain fear onto other people or situations. This was case during last century's so-called Cold War. And it continues to be the case with the terror wars that are currently enmeshing the entire human world. Certainly, there are people who want to control others and who are willing to terrorise, hurt, maim or kill if they can't do so. However, to see "reds potentially under every bed", to use the Cold War saying, is merely to project old brain fear onto current political reality. No matter how rational the justification may be, the fact remains that this century's terror wars are underpinned by fear manifesting in defensive behaviours. In effect, the everyday awarenesses of those individuals who are driving the political fear of terrorists have been captured by deeply buried instinctive old brain survival mechanisms. This is not to discount the behaviour of opportunists and cynics who manipulate others' deep-seated fears to achieve their own political agendas.

For those who seek to gain control of their body, psychological make-up, and everything else involved in the task of being a spiritual consciousness embodied in human reality, having everyday awareness captured by buried fear is a hugely limiting state. The reason is that if one's awareness is driven by buried fear, and so is occupied with all the self-defensive emotions, thinking and activities that fear gives rise to, no time, energy or space within one's awareness is left to focus on deeper matters—such as developing one's positive essence qualities, or attending to the tasks you, as a spirit, have chosen to engage in during this incarnation.

The disadvantage of living with an awareness driven by fear is plainly visible in the current planet-wide obsession with tracking terrorists. There are much graver issues for humanity as a whole to address, such as the impacts of over-population, factory fishing, the ways industrial agriculture is ravaging ecosystems, and climate change. But projected fear leads to terrorism having much more political attention and financial resources turned towards it than those other issues, despite the implications of these non-terrorism issues potentially being far more devastating both to humanity and to the planet's biosphere as a whole.

The point we are making here is that addressing fear is crucial, because purifying one's everyday awareness, and gaining clarity of perception, emotion and thought, is a necessary preliminary not only to being realistic about the state of one's environment, but to delving into one's deeper selves.

In this chapter we intend to identify a number of key types of fear that drive human interactions. These are not the only kinds of fear. Many others could be identified. But the purpose here is to give you, the seeker of self-knowledge, a range of conceptual tools by which to analyse your own and others' behaviour. Having these tools will enable you to arrive at an understanding of what parts of your human psychological make-up "play you false", leading you away from knowledge and growth by diverting your awareness into self-focused defensive behaviours.

THE SEVEN TYPES OF HUMAN FEAR

In the previous section we described how, over the course of the millennia, ancient old brain instinctive fear was socialised into culturally accepted forms of behaviour. At the individual level this process involved ancient primal fear becoming crystallized into commonly manifesting behavioral patterns. We here identify seven patterns of fear as key to understanding how human psychology functions. The seven crystallised fears are:

- The fear of not having enough
- The fear of being vulnerable
- The fear of missing out
- The fear of being inadequate
- The fear of being worthless
- The fear of losing control
- The fear of the new

It can readily be understood that these seven types of fear are centred on the biological and social levels of human existence.

Thus *the fear of not having enough* can be seen to be grounded in experiences of famine and starvation. As starvation has been a recurring event throughout human history, the human psychology has compensated by reaching out and grabbing whatever it can, hoarding more than it immediately requires in order to ensure it doesn't starve. With increased productivity through agriculture, the likelihood of starvation gradually diminished. Yet the by now psychologically imbedded behaviour of grabbing more than enough was transferred from food to property, possessions, slaves, status, and so on. Thus the fear of not having enough changed, over the millennia, from being directed towards collecting food to manifesting towards whatever was socially important to the individual concerned. Today this grasping to excess is called greed.

The fear of being vulnerable also has its origins in humanity's physical vulnerability during its hunter-gatherer phase, when there were few human beings, tribes were small, and wild animals were numerous and potentially deadly. Vulnerability needs a shield to protect its soft inner core. So these early human beings developed a psychological defensive shield that manifested as a warrior strut, projecting confidence and even aggression to hide the fearful and uncertain centre. This "warrior strut" became useful not only for facing down wild animals but also for facing down human aggressors.

Again, by the time the physical dangers posed by wildlife had diminished, this psychological self-protective shield had hardened into what today can be labelled arrogance. Arrogance once helped individuals survive in a dangerous world. Today arrogance is a commonly manifested psychological shield that protects the inner psyche that feels vulnerable and exposed.

The fear of missing out has its origins in both physical and social reality. There is a common saying that "the grass is always greener on the other side." This could be thought of as the mantra of those who fear missing out on what others have and that they feel they should have too. In a sense, it is similar to greed, insofar as it is focused on physically possessing, owning or controlling something. But it differs from greed in that greed grabs what is immediately at hand, or pursues what it doesn't have and brings it to hand, whereas the fear of missing out is focused on what is some distance away. In fact, it is often so far away it is never reached. This imbedded behaviour has crystallised into what today is called impatience. Where the greedy are terrified of starving to death, those who are impatient will in fact happily starve themselves in pursuit of what they fear they will miss out on.

The fear of being inadequate is entirely a function of human socialisation. In a group some feel themselves vulnerable, and that feeling expresses itself as a sense of being inadequate. Inadequacy is entirely an attitude of the socially conditioned self. It is often projected onto children by parents, although it may be religiously conditioned through doctrines such as original sin, which is designed to reduce believers before not only God but also before their supposed religious betters. When the fear of proving oneself inadequate is crystallised in the psychology, it manifests in the behaviour of self-deprecation. Self-deprecation can be interpreted as being humble or self-effacing, and so may be thought of as a virtue. However, when self-deprecation is a compensation for the fear of being inadequate it is no virtue at all. It is a psychological handicap.

The fear of being worthless is a subtle variation on the fear of being inadequate. However, it is somewhat more extreme. The feeling of being inadequate may be brought into this incarnation due to what has previously been experienced or may equally be conditioned during childhood. In contrast, the fear of being worthless is almost always carried over from a prior incarnation. It is used to work through deep-seated emotions, particularly self-undermining feelings of despair that gradually overtook that life. Correspondingly, it takes considerable effort to rise out of the fear of being worthless. As a crystallised behaviour pattern this fear manifests in martyrdom. The image of the fettered housewife who is a martyr to the wants of her children is a well-known example. Indeed, if her children are not particularly driven by wants she will project imagined wants onto them, then attempt to fulfil them. When her children reject her offerings, which is inevitable if they don't want to be crowded and if they have some zest and spikiness of their own, she will feel rejected and her sense of worthlessness will be reinforced. Some whistleblowers are driven by a sense of martyrdom. It may outwardly appear that their whistleblowing is extremely worthy, but, in fact, such individuals use their whistleblowing efforts to have themselves condemned, and in the process their feelings of worthlessness are reinforced.

The fear of losing control is experienced by a minority of people. However, it often has powerful repercussions. To compensate for their fear these individuals adopt strict codes of conduct. It may be a criminal code, adopted when the individual joins a gang. It may be a police code of conduct, adopted when joining the police force. Or it may be a religious or military code. The purpose is to use a self-selected external code of behaviour as a shield to cover up and hide the fear of losing control. If these individuals are happy to wholly surrender their volition to the external code, and if they remain subservient to the command structure of their adopted code, then they are safe. But for many of these individuals they also have a need to flirt with transgressing the code. This leads them to live double lives, such as the policeman who dabbles in taking or dealing drugs, or the highly respected member of the judiciary or government who uses prostitutes, or the married man who has a secret second family. When their transgression is discovered their world falls apart. This means that when the fear of losing control crystallises into its most negative form it manifests as self-destruction.

Each of these last three are socialised forms of fear. They have arisen as responses to conditioning or out of exaggerated responses to the difficulty of living with others. The seventh fear has its roots in the old brain world of reptiles and insects, but in its socialised form is somewhat more complex.

The fear of the new. When animals feel they are being stalked one common response, particularly in the reptilian world, is to freeze. Some insects and reptiles have skins that change colour to help them blend into their physical environment. In the human world there is a similar response when threatened. This is to freeze psychologically. The fear that generates this behaviour is the fear of the new. Within human culture, the new takes many forms. It may be that a new person, a stranger, arrives. Or that an individual has to enter a new group of people at work or play, or has to deal with a new and unfamiliar situation, which generates a fearful response. It may be that new methods or technology are introduced at work. For those possessed by fear of the new the response is to attempt to ignore the new person, situation or experience and carry on as before. Psychologically, this behaviour is known as stubbornness. It is an extremely common human behaviour, being deeply imbedded in the human psyche via the old brain. In fact, the fear of the new is the most common human fear, which makes stubbornness the most frequently encountered fear-based human behavioural trait. Stubbornness involves holding fast to the familiar, to the known, to the established, to what is decidedly not new.

THE SEVEN FORMS OF CRYSTALLISED FEAR

In summary, the seven basic human fears and their crystallised behavioural manifestations are:

- The fear of not having enough is crystallised into greed
- The fear of being vulnerable is crystallised into arrogance
- The fear of missing out is crystallised into impatience
- The fear of being inadequate is crystallised into self-deprecation
- The fear of being worthless is crystallised into martyrdom
- The fear of losing control is crystallised into self-destruction
- The fear of the new is crystallised into stubbornness

It can be seen from these descriptions that, in fact, in each case the fear has become buried under its outward behaviour. Thus the fear of not having enough becomes buried under the behaviour of being greedy. People readily perceive another being greedy, but they are oblivious to the fear that is driving that behaviour. Similarly, people see an individual being self-deprecating. They may even approve of the behaviour. But they certainly fail to perceive the fear of being inadequate that drives the outward manifestations of self-deprecation.

One way to understand these crystallised behaviours is to perceive that they are fundamentally self-defensive in nature. What are they defending? They are defending the fear that drives them. A fear that remains hidden. So the individual who fears feeling vulnerable defends him or herself by adopting the shield of being arrogant. And the individual who fears losing control adopts the defensive behaviour of conforming to some behavioural code, transgressing which eventually tips them over into self-destructive actions. This adoption of this psychological self-defensiveness culminates in the edifice of chief feature.

Which fear drives *your* behaviour? What are *you* covering up? What fear are *you* hiding? Because, naturally, we are not talking in the abstract here. We are discussing the psychological make-up of all human beings. Which includes you who are reading this book. Keep these questions in mind. We will return to them in due course.

CHAPTER 2

The Edifice of Chief Feature

NOTHING DISTURBS HUMAN BEINGS AS MUCH AS THE FEELING that they are being seen through. This is because there are layers on layers of protective strategies, attitudes and emotions within the everyday human awareness. And no one likes their protective layers being identified by others.

What are those layers protecting? Their own otherwise naked self. Without layers of protection, the human being would feel vulnerable and exposed in a world which can be extremely challenging, grating, caustic and, at times, outright dangerous, not only to individuals' continued physical existence, but particularly to their emotional and intellectual stability.

We refer here to human existence at the level of the biological, socialised and essence selves. At the spiritual level there is no need for these layers of protection because nothing in the human or natural world can injure the spiritual self. So, to be clear, we reiterate that it is the everyday human identity that contains layers of protective strategies, attitudes and emotions.

In normal parlance a protective layer is passive. That is, it functions as a coat or as the external cladding of a house, protecting the wearer or those inside the house from wet, cold or overly hot weather. In contrast, the protective layers within the human psyche are not passive. They are active. That is, they react to perceived threats and initiate evasive action. Sometimes this action is on the physical level and results in an attempt to avoid bodily threats. However, most evasive action occurs on the emotional and intellectual levels. This manifests psychologically in behaviours that are not passively protective, but are rather actively self-defensive.

Self-defensiveness takes many different forms. There is the desire to conform, in which individuals seek to defend themselves from being perceived as different. There is the dread of being left out, which leads individuals to align themselves to others who have arranged themselves into groups. There is the desire to blend in, which inhibits individuals from expressing themselves. There is the self-protective behaviour of attacking others, which is not to harm the attacked but to protect the attacking individual's frail sense of personal identity. There is the urge to open oneself up to being exploited, which is a form of inverse self-protection, the feeling being that if one opens oneself up one will be embraced and perhaps even loved.

All these behaviours, whether they involve an individual huddling in a corner far away from others or giving them full access to body or psyche, are equally forms of self-protection. And all self-protection emanates from a need to cope with whatever environment individuals find themselves in. In this sense, self-protective behaviours are elaborate coping mechanisms.

We observed in *Practical Spirituality* that coping mechanisms develop during childhood. Childhood is an extremely stressful period for most human beings. Family and social environment and conditioning forcefully and deeply imprint attitudes, concepts and emotions on a child's developing psyche and awareness. All contribute to the forging of social identity. During childhood each individual's own deeper essence level urges and desires also emerge, often battling it out with parental prohibitions and with peer exhortations to cross the line as the growing child seeks to find acceptable ways of giving expression to their essence level drives and desires. In the give and take, thrust and counter-thrust environments of household, schoolyard and the community, the acceptable is often breached. Reactions then occur. Along with consequences.

Thus children are faced with having to cope with many different, often contradictory urges, commands, prohibitions and goadings coming from both outside and inside them. With so much occurring around and to the developing child, it is only natural that he or she develops mechanisms to cope. These mechanisms are psychological and behavioural in nature. And they end up protecting individuals not only through childhood, but well into adulthood. Even till death.

Why do they remain in place for so long? Because, having been sustained for many years through the childhood and teen years, by the time an individual arrives at adulthood his or her everyday awareness has accommodated itself to those behaviours. They have become familiar protective armour. Seeing no need to shrug them off, indeed needing them in order to maintain a continuing sense of personal safety in an often fractious world, where private feelings are frequently no sooner exposed than they are trampled on, it is perfectly understandable that individuals maintain their functioning. Thus by adulthood these behaviours, which originally developed out of the child's need to cope, have crystallised into a hard shell of self-protection.

The advantage of a hard shell is that it prevents unwanted probing or impingement arriving from outside. The disadvantage of a hard shell is that it prevents soft, gentle and loving reaching from arriving from outside. And it also prevents the individual reaching out towards others in a soft, tender and loving way. Psychologically, self-protective behaviours become a prison that confines the individual's awareness to a narrow range of feelings, thoughts, attitudes, shared communications and experiences.

Clearly, this is to any individual's disadvantage. Enclosure confines awareness, preventing it from being open to new experiences, feelings, thoughts and understanding. Enclosure prevents growth. All kinds of flailing emotions then result, such as frustration, anger, resentment, self-pity. These emotions are manifestations of the sense of enclosure, as are feelings of entrapment and futility. Profound unhappiness and depression then arise. All this occurs because coping mechanisms and behaviours that developed during childhood have taken over an individual's everyday awareness and set up long-time residence there, building ever stronger walls and edifices.

An incredibly strong sense of personal identity accrues around this edifice of self-protective behaviours. This is adult crystallised social identity. And, of course, fear is buried right at the heart of it all.

FEAR AND CRYSTALLISED SOCIAL IDENTITY

Underlying all childhood behaviour is the fear of not being able to cope. Naturally, this is very rarely expressed consciously, because children don't have the degree of acuity that would enable them to identify and give voice to their deepest impressions and feelings. So instead of expressing their fear, they adjust themselves to minimise the perceived threat.

And we deliberately use the word "perceived" on the grounds that perception is actually more significant than reality. Why? Because for any ten children faced with the same threat, each will respond differently. Some won't perceive a situation as a threat at all. This could be to their advantage, because they happily sail past the threat without reacting. Or it could be to their disadvantage, because without them knowing what is happening the unperceived threat grabs them and pulls them under. Then there is the variability of human psychological make-up, by which a range of individuals respond very differently to the same experiences. Some shrug off threats that impact powerfully on others, to the extent that it lives inside them for the rest of their life. Others don't even perceive the danger of what they just walked by.

So childhood coping behaviours easily, automatically even, become unacknowledged inner reactions. Unrecognised and so ignored, they are then covered over as the awareness engages with ongoing everyday activities. Thus responses become buried, in the sense that the child's own everyday awareness is oblivious not only to what has occurred, but also to its own inward reaction to what occurred.

A perceptive adult may attempt to help the impacted child adjust, offering affirmations or quelling fears of not coping, in order to push or pull the child into another psychological state. But more usually a perceptive adult is not in a position to effect any psychological or behavioural change. Or no one notices at all. Consequently, because the unacknowledged coping behaviours help the child get through the hours, weeks and years, the child repeats those behaviours, usually unconsciously. In this way the coping behaviours become habitual. And as these repeated behaviours become intrinsic to the child's developing psyche, the originating incidents, reactions and coping mechanisms become buried ever deeper within the crystallising socialised self. By "buried deeper" we mean that the child, now likely a teen, looks at the world through the lens of its impacted everyday awareness., but is unable to see what is buried psychologically within the structure of its own perceptual and processing apparatus.

Yet this unseen lens profoundly affects its vision of the world. By adulthood, when the socialised self and its perceptions complete the crystallisation process, childhood fear-based coping mechanisms have formed an elaborate self-defensive structure. This structure provides the behavioural traits that are commonly called personality.

By way of example, one woman may be seen by others to have a shy personality, retiring whenever she is overwhelmed by people or situations, and it doesn't take much for her to feel overwhelmed. Another is known as the life of the party, but actually doesn't know when to stop, being afraid to go home and be alone, or alternatively not wanting to return to whoever is waiting there. Another is considered by friends to be somewhat stingy, but unknown to them regularly turns up at a favoured club, perhaps for decades, where she is a good tipper. Yet another is considered to be a great friend, opening her house to all and sundry.

Yet all these behaviours, which others perceive as positive or negative personalities that they enjoy being around or that they avoid, are actually ingrained adult expressions of coping mechanisms that go back to childhood. They are the manifestation of an individual's crystallised socialised self. They're not real and meaningful expressions of deep human nature centred on the essence self. They are compensating behaviours that have their basis in socially generated fear, which itself stimulated the formation of childhood coping mechanisms.

When we stated at the beginning of this chapter that nothing disturbs human beings as much as the feeling that they are being seen through, what we were referring to was the deep-seated fear of being exposed. Knowing that others can see that far into you is chilling, because it generates the feeling that your deepest secrets are open to external view. Even worse, admitting the validity of such perceptions forces individuals to confront their own most hidden fears. That is a profoundly disturbing experience.

Yet that it what we are about to ask you to consider. Every human being is beset by negative psychological traits. These traits create a psychological structure that in effect imprisons the human everyday awareness within hard-set behavioural bars. Everyday awareness then perceives in a narrow and limited way, looking at the world between those hard-set bars. The only way to free awareness is to demolish the psychological edifice. And the only way to do that is to confront and eliminate the central underlying fear.

Doing so is no easily accomplished task. Many people can't even bear to consider their fears, let alone actively acknowledge, confront and wrestle them. It could be said that this is one of the most difficult tasks anyone can carry out. Yet it must be done at some time or other, and repeatedly, over a large number of lifetimes, in order to progress towards becoming a knowing and loving embodied spiritual being.

We have already identified seven fears as key to human psychology. We now add that each gives rise to a psychological edifice of related self-defensive behaviours. This edifice we name chief feature.

IDENTIFYING THE EDIFICE OF CHIEF FEATURE

As we observed in the previous chapter, the socialisation of the seven fundamental fears has given rise to seven crystallised human behaviours. We are calling these crystallised behaviours chief features. They are *chief* features because they dominate an individual's psychological make-up. Each chief feature is grounded in its respective fear. Hence there are seven chief features that are psychological crystallisations of the seven underlying fears. These seven chief features are greed, arrogance, impatience, self-deprecation, martyrdom, self-destruction and stubbornness.

- The fear of not having enough is crystallised into greed
- The fear of being vulnerable is crystallised into arrogance
- The fear of missing out is crystallised into impatience
- The fear of being inadequate is crystallised into self-deprecation
- The fear of being worthless is crystallised into martyrdom
- The fear of losing control is crystallised into self-destruction
- The fear of the new is crystallised into stubbornness

The reason it is important to identify chief feature is that it forms the psychological edifice around and on top of which other self-defensive behaviours are arrayed. We have previously observed that the four principle forms of self-defensiveness consist of denying, justifying, deflecting and attacking.

Human beings use these behaviours to variously defend their perspective, their income, their possessions, their status, or their sense of entitlement. Yet, ultimately, denying, justifying, deflecting and attacking are strategies utilised to defend chief feature. And, in the process, to protect the fear that beats in the basement of the edifice that is their chief feature.

This is why nothing compares to the pain an individual feels on being confronted with the reality of their chief feature and with the exposure of their chief feature's manifestation in aggressive, slippery, obsequious, violent, nastily mischievous, self-pitying behaviours, or in the many ways that human beings deny, justify, deflect or attack others. This is why no one enjoys being confronted with their underlying fears, or facing up to childhood or adult incidents that have led to the construction of chief feature.

For chief feature *is* a construction, built piece by piece, over the years, until it has become embedded in the human psyche, *becoming so much a part of an individual's awareness that it is invisible to the individual's own perception because it is in-built into that perception.*

ADDRESSING CHIEF FEATURE

Of course, when individuals look at others they can often perceive parts of their self-defensive edifice. But they rarely see the complete structure. Digging into personal history is required in order to get at the incidents and fears that originally generated the coping behaviours on which the individual's psychological make-up is built.

Various psycho-therapeutic methods exist to help distressed individuals identify their personal coping mechanisms and adjust those mechanisms sufficiently to coexist with others without standing on their toes. Or worse. However, most psychological therapies and treatments have the aim of merely helping a distressed individual cope with everyday life. Such low level coping is not what we are striving to achieve here.

Rather, we are suggesting that anyone who is committed to spiritual exploration needs to address their own defensive behaviours, by identifying them, deconstructing them in the sense of coming to understand how they arose, and then actively working to break down the edifice of defensive behaviours built on them, piece by piece. Merely adjusting oneself to one's own emotional inadequacies is not enough. They must be eradicated.

In stating this we are conscious that to begin this depth of inner work you need to be reasonably well adjusted. So if you are in a stressed state, deal with the stress first. Only after a normal degree of equilibrium has been reasserted—normal, that is, for you—should you begin to carry out this deconstructive work. Additionally, what we are seeking to address here mustn't be confused with the need to deal with traumatic life events, for example losing your job, having a long term relationship or marriage end, losing a child, almost dying, being violently assaulted, or facing the consequences of a major transgression. These are all life events that can, and often do, tap into deep-seated fears. Each may radically change the direction of a life. But these are not what we are addressing here. What we are drawing attention to are long and deeply buried fears, that have their roots in childhood, and the attitudes, emotions and coping mechanisms they give rise to.

However, we do add the caveat that traumatic life events can certainly rip away the protective layers of the psyche, exposing deeply buried emotions and their fears to view. And, certainly, anything that throws you off-balance for a period, without being traumatic, can be very useful for exposing deeper feelings, motivations and memories of key childhood events, and so will help cast light into the murky depths of your psyche. In fact, this issue of being thrown off balance is crucial, because it is only at times when your everyday awareness is not entirely caught up in its own momentum, when its daily momentum is interrupted, that the opportunity arrives to shine a light within.

CHIEF FEATURE IS CHOSEN

In the previous book we offered an example of a man, Bill, who used criticism offered by others to re-evaluate his behaviour at work. His willingness to look at himself became a turning point that interrupted the automatic momentum of his everyday awareness. It ended up facilitating the realisation of his life plan. This is a common example of how individuals begin the demanding task of addressing their chief feature and its numerous and devious manifestations.

To add to that example, we could now say that Bill had a chief feature of arrogance. As noted above, arrogance is a coping mechanism that results from the fear of being vulnerable. Bill's vulnerability was itself embedded into him as a result of his relationship with his father. (Reviewing Chapter Seven of *Practical Spirituality* will further illuminate this point.)

However, Bill's arrogance was not accidental. Neither was Bill's central fear of being vulnerable. The spiritual identity who took on the sub-identity of Bill selected that fear and its chief feature prior to incarnating. Thus the relationship with an oppressive father, a relationship that generated the fear of being vulnerable, was chosen precisely so that the incarnating spiritual identity could work on a specific set of behaviours. This was all for the purpose of using those behaviours to further work through the psychological implications, for that individual spirit, of living in a human body.

This situation and its attendant fear was chosen because of what the spirit had experienced in previous incarnations. It selected both negative and positive traits, which it had developed in previous lives, and that it wished to confront and diminish in this incarnation. In general, chief feature is chosen prior to incarnation. However, (and, we note, only very occasionally) childhood situations do not always play out as planned and a different fear may come to dominate that sub-identity than what was selected. Whether chosen or arising unexpectedly, chief feature functions as a key obstacle to anyone seeking to develop their essence self's potential, let alone for those who wish to contact their spiritual self.

A triumph in any life involves confronting chief feature and diminishing, if not completely eliminating, the fear that underpins chief feature. Do that and much will have been learned about being a spirit incarnated in a human body.

DIGGING INTO FEAR

We have previously discussed the need to purify everyday awareness in order to perceive clearly and to develop one's inner potentials. We now extend the discussion on purification by stating that a major part of purifying oneself involves deconstructing the edifice of chief feature and its fear.

Deconstruction is a process that begins with self-observation. In Chapter Thirteen of *Experimental Spirituality* we suggested a process for observing oneself with the aim of identifying the fear, or fears, that lie buried in one's psyche as a result of childhood experiences. We suggest you review that process and carry out the exercise. With the data gathered as a result of doing so you will be in a strong position to identify your underlying chief fear.

Of course, other fears will likely also be apparent. So it will likely take an extended period of thinking and making further observations in order to identify your primary fear. A significant problem is that the first fears you identify are unlikely to be your key fear. The reason is that the key fear is the most deeply buried. So lesser fears—although certainly not less significant fears—will inevitably be discerned first.

We suggest you not discard those fears from consideration. Either make a note of them and carry on seeking to identify other more deeply buried fears, or address that fear and seek to identify what it comes from. It may have arisen from a trauma, be a conditioned response to repetitive negative stimulus, or be a relatively late addition to the layers of your psyche. It doesn't matter which. Working to identify any negative and self-limiting trait, no matter how shallow or deep, is good work and worth pursuing. And you can enjoy knowing that once one fear is identified, there is always another to dig up and mull over! Accordingly, there is always a need to follow a fear, or a negative or self-limiting behaviour or manifestation, back to its source. It may take weeks, or months, or even years to do so.

The first level is to follow whatever is being examined back to its origins in the socialised self. This inevitably involves re-examining childhood experiences and reactions. The origins of the key fear and its associated chief feature can always be traced back to childhood. Because that is when the foundations were laid on which your entire socialised self is built.

The second level is at the level of the essence self. In particular, within the moving, emotional and intellectual centres. Chief feature and its fear provide the foundations of the socialised self. But they also thread through the layers of the essence self. Often when you are alone and engrossed in an essence activity you bypass the socialised self. Consequently, your chief feature and its underlying fear are not engaged. But as soon as an essence level activity involves others, and especially when that activity is being performed in an occupational, family or social environment, the socialised self kicks in and there is a likelihood that defensive behaviours will start impacting on the essence self's work.

To take a simple example, a builder might be quite happy working in his essence self's moving centre. Then the boss appears, is in a stressed state, and severely criticises the builder's work. In response, the builder's defensive mechanisms manifest. His awareness shifts from the moving centre to welling emotions, and his characteristic psychological reactions, emanating from his chief feature and its underlying fear, come into play. Depending on how chief feature manifests, the builder may argue back, resign on the spot, moan at length to others, or lapse into sullen silence. He may even return to his work calmly, apparently unaffected. Naturally, just because he appears to return calmly to work doesn't mean he is not seething inside.

His reaction depends on how developed or undeveloped the builder is in his emotional centre, and how emotionally robust or unstable. If he is stable, he will be able to shrug off the boss' comments and carry on. But most human beings are unstableto some degree, so react. In doing so, their everyday awareness will shift into the negative aspects of their socialised self, and whatever resentments, anger, rage, self-pity or fears that normally reside there will rise in response to the boss' input. Such situations are actually excellent opportunities to identify a key emotion and follow it back to its source in the socialised or essence self, or both.

The third level to which emotions and their underlying fear may be traced is to prior incarnations. That is how deep-seated they often are. Naturally, the everyday awareness of your current sub-identity can have no knowledge of prior life experiences that are now manifesting in this life. Observations and analysis are insufficient to uncover these very deeply buried incidents. However, a clue is provided in cases where you trace an emotion back into childhood, and you then find no incident that appears sufficiently strong to have initiated it. This suggests the initiating incident occurred during a prior incarnation.

To hunt down emotions that have their source in prior incarnations you have to contact your spiritual self. This may be done in meditation, by posing questions. It may also be sought through dreams, by posing a question before going to sleep. Hypnosis may prove useful. Or, after focusing intensely on the issue for a period of time, the answer may spontaneously appear in your everyday awareness. In that case, concentration would have opened up a path to the spiritual self, via which it was able to tell you what you wished to know.

A COMMENT ON METHOD

It may seem that this is a somewhat roundabout method, even an overly slow process, for addressing underlying emotions and trauma. This is true. But it is also a safe method. And it ensures life lessons are learned and deep understanding is achieved.

Whenever childhood conditioning and trauma are explored emotional leakage, perhaps even major overflow, is involved. This is because in digging up buried emotions, those emotions enter the purview of the everyday awareness. And the everyday awareness will relive the experience, or the emotional aftermath of the experience, at least in part.

By adopting an analytical approach, these buried emotions are accessed via the intellect. And the intellect has built-in detachment. So the full brunt of the emotions will be blunted, so to speak, by being placed in the context of a wider intellectual understanding of how everyday identity came to be what it is. In this way the essence self's intellect keeps the socialised self's emotions and traumas at a distance and stops them flooding into the emotional centre and the whole process of remembering becoming traumatic all over again.

It is possible to approach this process in quite a different way. For example, some meditation-based and psycho-therapeutic practices can take one's everyday awareness directly into the emotional memory of traumatic childhood events. The idea is that by directly entering the buried and built-up emotions one can release them, in an exercise much like lancing a boil, letting out the emotional pus and poison.

This approach can certainly work. But if no analysis occurs, one is left without any understanding of what happened, how it happened, why it happened (and, as we have pointed, *why* can go very deep), how it shapes your everyday identity, and how that emotion now fits into the edifice that is your crystallised everyday identity with its dominating chief feature.

In addition, and this is a serious issue, if the boil is lanced, but the boil is the result of poor diet or vitamin deficiencies, then other boils will form. Similarly, if you lance a buried emotion, but do not understand how it came about and what behaviours feed it, and feed off it, and what compensating stabilising behaviours are generated by it, then the issue hasn't truly and fully been dealt with. The underlying fear remains untouched.

Chipping away at the edifice of crystallised chief feature may be slow. But it is sure. And, in the long term, it is effective.

CHAPTER 3

False Personality as Obstacle

I N *PRACTICAL SPIRITUALITY* WE OBSERVED HOW EVERYONE HAS A fundamental choice in life. You may choose to shift your everyday awareness into the momentum of the essence self as it strives to fulfil the life plan your spiritual self has selected for this incarnation, or you may keep your everyday awareness wholly immersed in the momentum of the crystallised socialised self. We now wish to add further detail to what shapes the crystallised social self, drawing on what has just been stated about fear and chief feature and adding the new concept of false personality.

In the previous two chapters we indicated the degree to which adult crystallised social identity is shaped by deeply buried fear and coping mechanisms developed during childhood. The result is the building of an edifice of defensive behaviours dominated by chief feature. It can be further stated that this adult crystallised social identity has a particular personality that has been shaped by fear and its chief feature. That personality we here identify as false personality.

False personality is fear-based. When an individual faces any choice there are two fundamental ways he or she may respond, two basic psychological momentums that may be engaged. Either the choice is made by the active parts of the essence self, and the individual consequently takes a path consistent with the blossoming of the life plan. Or the choice is made at the level of the crystallised socialised self, and the path is taken to continue defending the fear-based false personality.

False personality embodies the most negative and most limiting character and behavioural traits that exist within any individual's psyche. In the case of our hypothetical engineer Bill, when he was confronted by his own controlling and domineering behaviour, an observation that was actually an inner cue whispered by his own spiritual self, he had two fundamental ways in which he could have responded. In the first he could have automatically defended himself by abusing the complainers, reporting them, or walking out on the job. Such a self-defensive choice would have been made at the level of false personality. What he actually did was take the criticism on board, process it, and use it as a life lesson that helped him gain clarity about himself. That whole experience then became a turning point in his life, because he chose to use his essence self to respond to the external observation and its associated inner cue. Hence it could be said he responded from his true personality.

The result, as we saw, was self-transformation and significant inner growth. In contrast, when an individual's everyday awareness is centred in false personality, no growth occurs. Instead, daily life remains a pile-up of defensive reactions.

Of course, no life is entirely filled just with fear-based defensive emotions, thoughts and actions—even if the lives of children living in countries ravaged by constant war and famine are certainly nearly so. Rather, everyone has moments of respite when positive essence traits are to the fore, or when the socialised self is not engaged and therefore false personality is quiet. The problem is that when the pressure comes on, and especially at those times when a major turning point in a life is approached (and turning points tend to challenge and even threaten to tear apart the entire fabric of how the life is currently being lived), huge stress may be involved. The issue is that when individuals dominated by false personality become stressed, they automatically draw on the psychological template offered by false personality, so allowing its inbuilt fears and defensiveness to dictate what choice is made. Thus a significant inner cue is declined. And the crucial choice an individual's spiritual self organised prior to incarnation isn't taken up. The result is that a key opportuniy is wasted.

This is why we consider it is so crucial that any individual who wishes to understand the purpose of their life, and who wishes to engage with their spiritual self, addresses fear and chief feature. If this is not done there is a likelihood that opportunities your spiritual self wants you to pursue will be missed. And much less will be accomplished during the life than was available to be achieved.

CHOICE AND FALSE PERSONALITY

Of course, and as we have been at pains to point out in our previous missives, no life is wasted. Everything can and does provide life lessons. Ultimately, you will realise your potential in the ways you choose— with the emphasis being on "the ways you choose", because your life, your series of incarnations, and your spiritual self, they are all yours to do with as you decide. In the final analysis, there is no right or wrong way to explore the myriad opportunities provided by incarnation in the human domain. There is only what you choose to pursue, and what you choose not to pursue.

Our intention here is to help you maximise your choices and get the most out of any opportunity that presents itself. We want you to develop mastery. This is not because having mastery is better than not having mastery—although being highly competent at an activity certainly generates more options, which in turn makes a life more challenging, and plainly and simply generates greater fun. The point is that in the struggle to develop mastery you maximise what you learn and develop within yourself. As a result, you evolve as a spiritual identity. And becoming a more evolved spiritual identity is certainly rewarding in its own terms, because of the new possibilities it opens up.

In stating this, we observe that you, at the level of your ongoing spiritual identity, want to evolve. This is why you made the choice to engage in an extended series of incarnations in the human domain in the first place. You have "descended" into a body, and are currently "riding" it in self-selected ways, in order to evolve. So you, at your spiritual level, want to respond to inner cues, want to make use of turning points, want to draw life lessons, and want to gain mastery over the situation of being a spirit in a body.

The biggest single obstacle to this occurring is false personality.

STEPPING AWAY FROM YOURSELF

In the previous chapter we outlined an analytical approach to unpicking chief feature and its underlying fear. The same approach, indeed the same material, is required to unpick false personality.

But in order to unpick them you have to "get out of them". By this, we mean you have to shift the centre of your everyday awareness from your so-cialised self to your essence self. When you live more of your life in your essence self you will accomplish several things:

- You will have more focus to develop your essence self's positive traits and purify it of negative traits.
- You will short circuit false personality, because by not engaging with your socialised self you will not automatically get caught up in its self-defensive behaviours.
- You can develop in your everyday awareness a greater sense that you, as an individual, are not wholly situated in and identified by your childhood situations, conditioning and trauma.

Being in your essence self, that is, living in a state in which your everyday awareness is centred in your essence self, you can develop an appreciation of the fact that while past events and your reactions to those events are certainly part of you, they do not define you. They have contributed to what you are. But they are far from being all that you are.

Developing an ability to "step away from yourself", not just to spend quiet periods disengaged from the momentum of everyday life, but to spend periods disengaged from the constant inner whirring of your everyday perceptions, emotions and thoughts, is crucial to developing a deepening sense of your self. You have many layers. You go a long way down (or up, if that is your preferred metaphor). But in order to plunge into those depths (or fly into those heights) you need to let go. You need to let go of the superficial levels of your own self. Then you will learn many wondrous things.

The problem is, the shallower parts of your own layered self don't want to let go of your awareness. They hang on. Often when people begin meditating they experience fear. They think this fear is their fear. That isn't the case. In fact, it is fear generated by false personality because it doesn't want to be left behind. This is a very significant point. *The fear isn't your fear.* It is the fear of your false personality. And false personality is a by-product of the process by which a spirit enters a body and steers it through the multiple difficulties that comprise the human domain.

We repeat, *the fear is not your fear.* So step aside from it. Whenever fear arises, find a place within your essence self that isn't fearful. Stand in that place and examine the fear like a piece of food on the end of a fork. Turn it over. Examine it from all sides. Realise the truth that "this is not me".

Being able to inwardly step away from a situation, from a personal reaction, from an emotion, from a thought, and wonder where it came from, how it has manifested, and what kinds of behaviours it gives rise to, is all important work.

Indeed, this work is crucial to short-circuiting the otherwise circuitous workings of false personality and ensuring your life journey progresses in the direction you have chosen.

FALSE PERSONALITY MUST BE ADDRESSED

To recapitulate: False personality is a wholly self-constructed edifice. It is constituted of key psychological traits that you have chosen because you wish to address them in this life. At the same time, false personality and its traits are an obstacle that prevent you from engaging with your essence self and with your life goals and life plan. So by addressing false personality, by confronting your deepest fears, by grappling with defensive behaviours, and by deconstructing chief feature, you perform two tasks.

First, you overcome negative and self-limiting traits that have been bothering you, perhaps for a number of incarnations. Thus you purify your everyday self-awareness and progress towards purging contaminating behaviours and attitudes from your socialised self.

Second, you shift the focus of your everyday awareness from the momentum of your socialised self to the momentum of your essence self. This is crucial to carrying out the tasks you have set yourself this time round.

We will have more to say about how false personality disrupts a life journey in Part Four. Those chapters will illuminate in greater detail what constitutes false personality and how it diverts your everyday awareness into negativity and into making self-limiting choices. However, here we conclude this exposition of the ugly triumvirate of fear, chief feature and false personality, and progress to a consideration of what constitutes true personality and contributes to its growth. But first, we need to consider what growth involves.

PART TWO

CONDITIONS FOR GROWTH

CHAPTER 4

The Complexities of Choice

B EFORE WE CAN DISCUSS TRUE PERSONALITY AND ITS ASSOCIATION
with the essence self, we need to discuss the nature of growth. Growth
is a complex process. It involves multiple factors that interact on many levels.
In this and the next two chapters, we will introduce a number of concepts
that are basic if you wish to understand the what, how and why of human
growth. As always, these aspects are considered within a reincarnational
context. We'll begin by identifying three principles fundamental to growth:
choice, options and experience.

THREE BASIC PRINCIPLES FOR GROWTH

In any life choice is fundamental. This is the first basic principle. Choice applies before a life is lived and during the course of living that life. The essential elements of any life are chosen. The purpose behind the act of choosing
is to provide optimal conditions for an individual spiritual identity's psychological growth and for it to develop specific skills, abilities and talents that are
expressions of its innate core disposition.

By optimal conditions we mean optimal for a particular spiritual identity at that particular phase of its evolution. Choices made at one time will
not be repeated at another. In situations where specific life circumstances
are apparently repeated from one life to another, new factors will play into
the latest circumstances. The second time the spiritual identity will have different aims and different developmental outcomes. As a result the individual

49

has quite different experiences to previously. Choice requires options. That everyone has options is the second basic principle.

Prior to incarnating, a number of options are laid out for the soon-to-be-embodied spiritual identity. Options may be complex or simple, coarse or subtle, easily comprehended or not obvious at all. What applies on the everyday human psychological level equally applies on the spiritual level: on each level, identities can never comprehend all the implications of the options that face them. Why not? Because of experience, the third key principle.

EXPERIENCE IS ALWAYS NUANCED

Spiritual identities not only exist at different levels of experience, but within each level the specific content of different identities' experience varies enormously. For example, in a class of six year old children, the overall average level of life experience is what is normal for six year olds. This level of life experience is very different from that possessed by nine or twelve year olds. So we can appreciate levels of experience demarcate six years from nine or twelve.

Yet within each of these levels individual children have very different kinds of experiences. Focusing now on just the six year old level, one child may be doing ballet classes, another taking musical lessons, and yet another could love tinkering in the garage with her Dad. Some read avidly, others love sport, others are natural story-tellers, yet others like to organise their friends or to follow. Innate propensities, ultimately manifestations of each individual's core spiritual identity, lead to different kinds of experiences being perceived as attractive and so selected and embraced

In addition, six year olds have very different home lives. The wealth or poverty of parents, the differing psychological make-ups of family members, and the ways family members interact, add another layer of psychological experience. For some, life circumstances are very tough. Others lead comparatively sheltered lives. Some lack basic levels of nutrition and health. Children are loved or not so loved. All these external factors enhance or diminish, help flower or cut off, the innate core drives.

A third layer of experience is how each child responds psychologically to their home situation, to family and friends, and to their wider social environment. As we have pointed out in the previous books in this series, inner reactions, which take the form of coping behaviours, generate a significant layer of experience.

Hence, in a classroom full of six year old children, most share a common developmental norm, enabling a visitor to their classroom to clearly differentiate them from nine and twelve year olds. Yet within the overall normative level of six year old experience, the actual content of personal experience varies enormously between individual children. So significant is the variation of personal experiential contact that, in fact, no two six year olds are the same. This applies equally to spiritual identities.

HOW PRIOR EXPERIENCES INFLUENCE CHOICE

The level of experience possessed by those who have incarnated sixty times differs from those who have incarnated ninety or one hundred and twenty times. And within these separate levels, what each spiritual identity has experienced also varies enormously.

This means that when a group of individuals who have each previously incarnated sixty times prepare for their next life, they are faced with different options. Overall, they have to deal with what is typical of those who have just sixty lives under their belt. For six year old children, the principle task consists of learning to live among other human beings, which involves learning to accommodate their identity and desires to the norms accepted by the community in which they are growing up. Similarly, those who have lived sixty lives are still learning the rules of human existence and how to accommodate their personal drives to human circumstances. Furthermore, just as six year olds have not experienced the subtle levels of adulthood, in fact have no idea of what the pleasures and pressures of adulthood actually involve, so those who have just sixty lives under their belts have limited perceptions of what is occurring around them. In particular, the subtleties of human thought and emotion remain unknown.

So at the experiential level of sixty lives it can be appreciated that all soon-to-be-incarnated spiritual identities are working from a common expe-

riential base. In broad terms, the options available to such identities have to
do with providing them with opportunities for adding to their stock of experiences. But focusing those broad options is another finer, more subtle sub-
level of options, which relate to each individual's prior experiences. What
exactly these more finely focused options consist of depends on what identities have experienced before, what they haven't experienced but wish to
experience, and on what experiences they wish to repeat in order to do them
better, or even just differently, compared to what they did before. In addition, every individual has had certain prior experiences that inhibited their
interactions with others and other experiences that they found satisfying and
that helped them grow.

These prior experiences narrow their focus when they consider all the
options available to them for living their next life. Prior experiences lead to
certain options being perceived as desirable and other options as not being
desirable. Thus, out of the entire range of possible options available to them,
individuals select those options that are perceived as most advantageous to
their growth at that particular phase of experience.

LEVELS OF OPTION-TAKING

Once these options are identified, yet another level of option-taking applies.
This is with respect to how an individual wishes to realise the chosen option
or options.

For example, an identity may be attracted to two sets of options, involving the fields of music and horticulture respectively. The identity, having experienced both fields in prior lives, now wishes to further develop sensitivity
and skills in each of these two fields. But there are options as to how they may
be explored. One option is to plunge into one field for several lives in order
to come to grips with all that it involves, then do the same for the other field.
A second option is to enter one field in the next life, and the other in the following life, consecutively bringing skills developed in one field to the other,
life by life. A third option is to adopt music as a profession and horticulture
as a hobby, or visa versa. A fourth option is to begin with music as a career,
then change careers and take up horticulture halfway through the life. Or,

again, visa versa. Then there are different roles within each: student, teacher, travelling expert, researcher, advance explorer or defender of orthodoxy.

Hence within the options provided by music and horticulture there are many sub-options. When first identifying broad options and then choosing which sub-option (or sub-options) it wishes to utilise, an identity draws on its experience. Using what it has previously undergone, the identity selects experiences it wishes to undergo not just in the immediate next incarnation, but within a series of incarnations—because it takes practice to achieve anything worthwhile. In this way experience, options and choice are interlinked principles that apply to each and every spiritual identity at each and every phase of its existence, both prior to incarnating and while living in a body and exploring chosen options.

Of course, this is a very simplistic presentation of the options identities face before they incarnate. To indicate what other issues are involved, we will briefly discuss how the desire to develop skills affects identifying and choosing options.

DEVELOPMENT AND CHOICE

Any skill has many levels extending from novice to mastery. Furthermore, mastery is never achieved in a single lifetime. One has to return to the same discipline again and again in order to experience all the nuances it contains. In the case of music, developing mastery of an instrument is just a basic level. Developing insights into the nature of music, and beyond music into the creative process in itself, introduces progressively deeper levels of mastery. Learning how to communicate your insights involves yet another level of mastery. Teaching others to explore their own instrument, music and creative process is another level again.

To continue our example of the option of simultaneously exploring music and horticulture, spending time in horticulture may be selected on the grounds that the individual decides it is a necessary adjunct to exploring the multiple nuances of music. Perhaps this is because music is personal and focused on oneself and one's personal expression, while plants exist externally to oneself. Appreciating how living beings interact with their environments, survive and grow may be perceived as offering valuable lessons regarding alternative (and notably impersonal) ways that creativity occurs. Such an experience may also provide important lessons on serving other beings, becoming self-effacing, learning to act as circumstances require, and generally learning to direct and sustain awareness away from oneself and one's desires.

The same process may equally apply to a spiritual identity who wishes to focus on horticulture, but takes up the option of also exploring the field of music in order to bring music-related lessons to the task of nurturing plants. Options provided by a secondary field, and the lessons learned there, almost always prove valuable to developing expertise in the field to which one is principally attracted. Psychologically, learning in a secondary situation, in a field in which one is not so personally and intensely invested, can be extremely beneficial. This is because, as the saying goes, the pressure is off, and the individual is able to learn in a more relaxed way. So for the individual who really wishes to became a master musician, spending a life or two working in horticulture can be helpful in letting the pressure off oneself. Learning still continues in this secondary field, but in a more low-key fashion. Then when the individual feels ready to return to its principal love, it has new skills, and especially a more relaxed demeanour, to bring to the life.

However, and this is an important point, the individual mulling the options of music and horticulture is highly unlikely to perceive the multi-level experiential benefits of entering those fields before they are experienced. In the same way that the six year old cannot know what he or she will feel like or know at the age of twelve, so spiritual identities choosing to explore any field of human endeavour for a series of lives in order to enhance particular skills, with the goal of ultimately developing mastery in an aspect of that field, cannot know how they will feel throughout the process or what they will have learned at the end of the process.

This also means that spiritual identities can only find out whether a particular field is really for them, and if so how they may best explore it, by doing it. Second-guessing beforehand doesn't work. This is how choice and experience interlock with option-taking. The future is unknown. The identity you will become as a result of the choices you make, and what you will experience as a result of selecting one option over another, is unknown.

Knowledge of outcomes only occurs one increment at a time, by living out your chosen series of incarnations.

The experiences you accrue as a result of repeated incarnation, and the lessons you draw from your experiences, feed your personal evolution. They make you what you become, because everything you experience and learn from will permanently pulse within your core as a spiritual identity. This is what entering a human body is all about. It is an extended process of repeatedly experiencing, learning, growing and, ultimately, evolving. Identifying options, choosing those that are most appropriate, and experiencing what is chosen, are the key principles that facilitate this process.

To repeat a statement we made previously, within human existence the place where options are recognised, where choices for growth are made, where experiences accrue, and where lessons are learned, is within the essence self.

A WORD OF CAUTION

As an addendum, we need to observe that the above comments on identifying options and making choices is very much simplified. In fact, many more pragmatic aspects and psychological issues are taken into account when the circumstances of a forthcoming incarnation are being planned. It would be tedious in the extreme to list all the various components that are involved in identifying manifold options and in working through the reasons options are either taken up, rejected, or put on hold for future incarnations.

And even if we were able to successfully list everything involved, it would still be a futile exercise. This is because the intellect associated with the embodied human everyday awareness is too limited to grasp all the possibilities simultaneously—that is, in comparison to the intellect of the non-embodied spiritual identity, which has a breadth and depth of perception and processing that is, simply, inconceivable at the level of the everyday human mind.

Accordingly, the above description of identifying and selecting options must be viewed as indicative only. The process at the level of spiritual identity is far more layered, subtle, expansive and, frankly, fascinating (at least for those who, like us, are drawn to delve at depth into the intricacies of growth as it plays out in the human domain), to be dealt with here in anything approaching the intricacy that is actually involved. Nonetheless, this is sufficient to indicate the complexities of choice that lie behind any life, even those that appear very uncomplicated from the outside.

Having discussed choice, option-taking and experience in general terms, we will now shift focus and examine how growth occurs more particularly at the level of the essence self.

CHAPTER 5

Skills, Abilities, Talents

I N PREVIOUS BOOKS IN THIS SERIES WE HAVE DISTINGUISHED
between growth and evolution. We have asserted that growth occurs within the essence self while evolution occurs at the level of the spiritual identity. This differentiation is necessary, because as a result of living through an average of one thousand incarnations the spiritual identity becomes much more than it was. It develops from naïve to experienced, from timorous to loving, from ignorant to knowledgeable. In all this it evolves. Particularly, it evolves from simple consciousness to complexly layered consciousness. By this process the spiritual identity becomes much, much more than it was before it began incarnating into human bodies.

In contrast, the essence self of an incarnating identity can only ever grow from seed to maturity. Throughout that life it remains limited to the"seed", that being the physiological, psychological, intellectual, genetic and social parameters it was born into. Unlike the spiritual identity, the essence self can grow to maturity within these parameters, but it can never become more than what it was at the start of that life. It is on these grounds that we differentiate between growth and evolution.

Yet essence level growth is required for spiritual evolution to occur, because spiritual evolution draws on and encompasses the essence level growth that occurs within each life. Imagine how much essence material is generated by spiritual identities as they experience and process a thousand or more lives! When all that experience is amassed, boiled down, and its essential qualities extracted, it is a heady brew, too rich and intense for any single human mind to apprehend. That "heady brew" is literally the experiential quintessence of everything a spiritual identity undergoes through its repeated cycles of essence level growth.

Just as three broad principles provide the conditions for growth in general, so there are three categories that may be used to identify growth within the essence self. These consist of skills, abilities, and talents.

DEVELOPING SKILLS

Skills are basic to achieving anything. A baby has to learn the skills of walking and talking. Without self-locomotion an individual cannot be an independently functioning human being. Without the ability to communicate, the individual is cut off from everyone else. For those born with impaired legs, or who are unable to hear or speak, technology has been developed to help them overcome their body's physical limitations so they may have self-location and be able to communicate. This technology is provided because it is recognised that without these skills the individual cannot function at a basic human level.

In educational circles, much childhood learning is focused on developing cognitive skills. Every animal and insect species has its own particular cognitive skills, basic to its functioning as a member of that species. The complexity of these cognitive skills depends on the complexity of the central nervous system and its associated brain. Because the human nervous system and brain are complex in comparison to other earth species, there are many skills to learn. Indeed, no one uses all the potentially available human cognitive skills, let alone utilises them to their maximum.

The extensive variety of their cognitive skills makes human beings very adaptable. They enable the blind to learn to "see" through their fingertips or ears. This wide range of cognitive skills has historically enabled human beings to survive in extremely testing environments.

The limbic system additionally contributes to the richness of human interactions. The limbic system is broadly associated with emotional states, including primitive emotions such as fear, pleasure and anger, and various drives, including sex, dominance and submission, and nurturing offspring.

Over the millennia the limbic system's emotions and drives have been socialised into many kinds of sophisticated behaviours, such as the ritualistic.

The need to develop social skills provides another huge field for human learning. Learning how to live with others is, as the developmental jargon goes, a massive learning curve. To offer just one example, there are many different social roles and many ways of playing those roles. (Refer to *Practical Spirituality* for a discussion of roles). It takes numerous lives to taste all the available roles. More are required to experience each at both the giving and receiving ends of roles. Further lives are needed to work through the consequences of errors of judgement and behaviour while engaged in particular roles, repairing mistakes and learning to play each role lovingly and knowledgeably.

From this example of roles, it can be appreciated that developing social skills is an ongoing process, learned in each and every life. To explicate this process by way of a metaphor, every child begins with learning to play in the sandpit with others, without throwing out anyone's toys or getting into fights. As they mature, individuals progress to overseeing others playing in the sandpit. They then move on to working collectively to build new sandpits for fresh generations of children. Given the range of complex psychological interactions that occur on the social level, the acquisition and development of social skills is is absolutely necessary for achieving ongoing growth.

This same principle applies to all basic skills. No one can develop within the human domain without them. They are basic to living as a human being.

LEARNING TO LIVE IN A BODY

When spiritual identities first incarnate their initial task, before they can do anything else, is to learn how to function within a human body. This is not easily done. Being inside a human body is an intense experience. The human brain's cognitive capacities are complex. So are human social environments. It takes repeated incarnations for a spiritual identity, and a naïve and inexperienced spiritual identity at that, to learn how to function within the human body and to live within human social environments.

Just as six year children are unaware of the complexities of adult behaviour occurring around them, so a newly incarnated spirit has not yet connected with all the complex functioning offered by its human brain's cognitive faculties. Not yet able to access these faculties, the naïve embodied spirit remains unaware of the subtleties of motive and desire driving those they interact with. Simply, these others are utilising much more of their own cognitive capacities. And they are able to do so because they are more experienced, and as a result of their experiences have developed more skills germane to the art of incarnation.

Children need a nurturing environment in order to develop their cognitive skills. If they are living in an abusive home situation, or in a traumatising social environment, they remain behaviourally inhibited. As a result they don't learn all the same cognitive and social skills other children learn as a normal part of growing up. Similarly, for newly incarnated individuals the intensity and complexity of sensory, hormonal and emotional input is such that they automatically feel somewhat abused. This is an entirely natural response to the intensity of what they are experiencing. Incarnation remains a traumatic experience for many individuals for many lives. As a result, because they feel so inhibited, at first they learn slowly. This manifests in behaviour that displays limited cognitive and social skills. It is only after a number of lives, which we could nominally put at sixty, that an incarnated spiritual identity has experienced and learned enough to start functioning as a normal human being—acknowledging that "normal" is a generalisation, and that in fact most people diverge in small or substantial ways from any so-called norm.

This cycle of being inhibited, learning to cope, gaining sufficient self-confidence to extend oneself, and beginning to explore the possibilities available in one's environment, is repeated in each and every life. The advantage for those who have incarnated more often is that in each incarnation they tend to become comfortable with their situation sooner in their life, solely because they have gone through the various phases of human existence more frequently. Having experienced childhood many times previously, including having experienced most of the stresses and traumas that typically occur during childhood, they are less thrown by negative inputs. In effect, undergoing repeated and various life experiences makes them more resilient.

What makes them resilient is that they have learned to detach their awareness from complete reliance on external stimuli. They have developed their inner resources. These inner resources exist at the level of their essence self. This brings us to the issue of abilities.

DEVELOPING ABILITIES

When a spiritual identity incarnates for the very first time in a human body, it is a blank slate as far as human skills are concerned. It will have developed certain skills already, during its unembodied existence. However, as with a human baby, these spiritual level skills are still rudimentary. They are what it needs in order to survive in spiritual level reality. It then takes on the task of human embodiment in order to enhance those basic spiritual level skills. As we noted earlier, a spiritual identity takes on the task of serial embodiment in the human domain with the aim of growing as a human being. That human level growth directly contributes to the identity's spiritual evolution.

So when a spiritual identity first incarnates in a human body, it is a blank slate on the human level. Anything is possible. It could become anything it wishes to be. As the saying goes, the world is its oyster. But from a spiritual perspective it is not entirely a blank slate. As we just observed, it possesses rudimentary spiritual level skills. In practice, these skills initially have minimal influence on what happens to the identity during its first incarnations. This is because, again as we have just stated, the experience of being in a body and engaging with the rough and tumble of human interactions is initially traumatic. The intense visceral quality of bodily experience overwhelms the naïve spirit. Whatever skills it has developed at the spiritual level are simply swamped.

However, after it overcomes its initial trepidation and finds its feet, it starts being attracted to some experiences over all the others that are available. The attraction occurs due to the spiritual identity's drive to express its own core disposition. In *Practical Spirituality* we attempted to convey the complex nature of core disposition. The fact that each spiritual identity possesses a primary disposition that is further modulated by modality and a secondary disposition means that, from a spiritual perspective, each newly incarnating individual is not a blank slate. Each has an innate predisposition that, when the individual learns to quieten its biological and socialised selves sufficiently, expresses itself within the individual's everyday awareness, pushing it to choose experiences that are satisfying to its innate core nature.

This drive towards achieving core nature satisfaction kicks in after just a handful of lives. The result is that at the same time as an individual is learning to cope with the hormonal drives of its biological self, and is also learning to use its cognitive facilities and to develop its social skills, it is simultaneously negotiating with its environment as its seeks out opportunities to express its innate nature. For example, if the individual has a core disposition of warrior, modulated by the introspective and expressive modes, and has a secondary disposition of servant, then that spiritual identity will seek out specific opportunities in which to give expression to that particular core make-up. This will be the case throughout all its lives, from first to last.

But human existence is complex. The incarnating identity will make mistakes. Lessons will be learned. From time to time (we are talking lives here, not years) it will impinge on others. Others will impinge on it. Self-limiting and negative behaviours will have to be faced up to, worked through, and overcome. Basic skills will be developed to higher levels of proficiency, and new skills learned. Yet all this is ancillary to the overriding goal: to use the opportunity provided by repeated incarnation to grow in the human domain. This growth has two fundamental aspects. The first is that it involves the growth of abilities that are manifestations of an identity's core propensities. The second is that the growth of those abilities occurs at the level of the essence self.

In using the word "abilities" in this way, we are deliberately differentiating it from skills. We have already defined skills as basic to existence in whatever domain one occupies. Thus spiritual skills are basic to surviving in the spiritual realm, while human motor, cognitive and social skills are basic to surviving in the human realm. Every time one enters a new field of endeavour and experience there are new skills to be learned that enable one to function at even a rudimentary way in that field. For example, one might be an expert violinist, and carry that expertise from life to life. But if one then becomes a builder, one needs to learn to use a hammer and saw. These are new basic skills. Without them one cannot build. So there are always new basic skills to acquire.

Abilities are skills taken to the next level. They result from focused endeavour. People are initially motivated to develop basic skills because they need them in order to function as a human being. Hence children are eager to learn to ride a bicycle or skateboard because of the further opportunities these skills provide, whether to socialise with friends, compete, or translate what is learned to another activity, such as riding motorbikes or surfing. When adults take up a new field of endeavour they are similarly eager to learn the skills fundamental to that field so they may progress in it. Serious application then leads to those skills becoming deeper abilities. Ultimately, individuals work to develop skills into an ability because they feel it is in their interests to do so.

It could be said that skills are acquired from necessity whereas abilities are developed from propensity. It is clear that different people have differing abilities. Some are wonderful musicians, some are creative constructors, some are sensitive gardeners, some are subtle accountants, some inspiring teachers, and so on. In fact, there are too many human abilities for anyone to master them all, even in two thousand lifetimes. In practice, individuals choose certain areas of expertise over others and focus their efforts there. What propels them to chose one field of expertise over another, and to approach that field in one way rather than another, is the predilection innate in their core disposition.

To repeat: Abilities are the human level manifestation of the spiritual core disposition as it selects a trajectory through a series of human incarnations. These abilities are self-chosen and developed by an individual as it lives life after life. They manifest on the essence level in the context of practical, emotional and intellectual endeavours, in fields such as sports, management, art-making, engineering, botany, mathematics, nursing, education, and so on. Whereas skills are basic to everyday human interactions, abilities are basic to specialised areas of human endeavour. The farmer, the scientist, the economist, and the chef each display specialised abilities that are significantly more complex than basic motor, cognitive and social skills. Individuals develop abilities in particular areas not by chance, but because they are drawn to them and possess sufficient passion for them to spend the time and energy necessary to develop them.

ESSENCE ABILITIES AND PASSION

To speak generally yet again, people are motivated to develop their abilities in a particular field of endeavour because something in it ignites a fire within. They feel a passion to become involved in it. Often, the source of this passion is inexplicable. For some, a passion burns in them from the time they are young, and everyone around that individual expects them to go into engineering, or chefing, or horticulture, or a sport, or whatever it is that their passion drives them into. For others, the passion flares unexpectedly, at an unlikely period of their life, and they feel driven to enter that field, make their mark in it, and develop expertise. Passion ignites in these different ways as a result of a drive emanating from the core disposition.

Two caveats need to made in relation to this last statement. The first is that many people enter a career, and even develop a modicum of ability, without a deep level of passion being involved. People are often pushed into occupations they are not particularly attracted to by family or by circumstance. For such individuals to develop the high levels of abilities we are alluding to here, they will have to ignite a passion within their life circumstances. In practice, many people faithfully carry out their required work, then direct their passion into their own family, or into a hobby, or into community activities. Thus money-earning occupations or careers are not the exclusive domain within which people develop abilities. Far from it. But it is certainly the case that without a degree of passion no abilities will flower to their fullest.

The second caveat is that people can lose the passion they had for working in or experiencing a particular field of endeavour that they were drawn to when they were younger. What has happened is that they have lost their essence level engagement with what they are doing. Instead, the activity has become physically rote or socially driven. In such a situation individuals need to change gear. By this we mean they need to re-engage, at a deeper level, with what they are doing. Alternatively, they may need to move into another, quite different field, one that does engage them at an essence level. Changing gear is necessary because the repetitions of daily life require significant focus and energy, and this constant outflow of energy can leach away one's enthusiasm for what previously was exciting. Such repetitions disrupt one's deeper connection with what one is doing. What is required is for individuals to open up a connection between their everyday awareness and their essence self and re-engage with their essence-level passion.

For newly incarnated identities, the problem tends to be too much external intensity. That is, they feel their own essence-level passion but, not yet being very skilled, they are unable to deal with the complex negotiations required to enable essence level drives to successfully manifest in multi-layered socially constructed environments. For those who have incarnated many times a common problem is insufficient internal intensity. This occurs because they have surrendered to the humdrum, familiar, and non-threatening social environment in which they live. (Clearly, in this last case we are talking of those privileged not to be living in life-threatening environments.) Everyone possesses essence level passion and intensity. An inner change of gears may be required from time to time to reconnect with it and recharge one's engagement with the essential circumstances of one's own life.

DEVELOPING TALENTS

A bullet derives its momentum from the gun from which it is shot. A spirit derives its momentum from its own desire to experience, learn and evolve. But different spirits possess different degrees of intensity. So they progress with differing kinds of intensity through the trajectories of their lives. Note we say "different kinds of intensity". This must be understood in the same way that flowers may be said to possess different shades of colouring. You may personally prefer one shade over another. But there is no hierarchical scale that identifies one shade as inherently better than another. They are just different, no less and no more. Similarly, different spirits, at their core, possess different kinds of intensity. No intensity is inherently better or worse than another. They are just what they are.

In the discussion of abilities, we introduced the word "passion" to reflect this fact of innate intensity. Everyone has passion. (Anyone who claims they don't have any passion, or that they used to when they were younger but now that passion has lapsed, are avoiding engagement with their essence self—they have surrendered to their false personality's defence mechanisms.) As will be clear from the above, the quality of any spirit's passion must change from life to life, reflecting experience and development. As one evolves from life to life, focus becomes different, one's motivating intent is different, and the width and depth of experience that one is able to cope with is different.

If false personality dominates in a life, passion is repressed. Alternatively, if the essence self is brought into active presence within the everyday awareness, then passion positively bursts out. Passion applied consistently leads to the development of abilities. When those abilities align with what is innate within the core disposition, passion flowers as talent.

At this point it would be useful to comment on passion in relation to the model of the five-layered self.

THE INTRICACIES OF PASSION

Biological passion manifests in the context of sex, reproducing, establishing personal territory, and nest-building. Parents' biological passion (which develops into much more than just the biological) manifests in their willingness to fight, even to die, to protect their children. Passion at the level of the socialised self manifests in social interactions and perceptions and includes sustained commitment to career, appearance, status, and reputation. Passion at the level of the essence self manifests in focusing one's abilities in fields of endeavour that enable one to express oneself practically, emotionally and intellectually. The energetic self, being a medium, has no passion of its own, but does possess its own particular colour and intensity. The passion of the spiritual self manifests in its pursuit of bliss.

At each level people also display certain talents. However, when a talent is displayed at the biological and social levels, this talent is not emanating from either the biological or socialised self. Rather, it originates in the essence self. Thus if an individual displays a natural talent for a particular sport, that person possesses a high baseline level of physical skill, but that skill is augmented by essence level abilities. So an individual may be able naturally to catch and throw a ball, but so can many other players. An individual stands out as talented because their basic motor skills are augmented by game savvy and by being able to perform at a much higher than normal level. Abilities become a talent as a result of sustained work, which is itself fuelled by passion emanating from the essence self.

Similarly, if someone has a talent for fashion, or for communicating, or for nurturing others, they are functioning at the socialised level, but the above average abilities they bring to what they do is an expression of their essence self. Social learning certainly facilitates the development of their talent, but they are adding much from their own practical, emotional and/or intellectual capacities. And essence level passion is behind it all.

Some individuals are considered to possess a freakish level of ability. They are a rare talent. Their abilities are called freakish because there seems to be no reason for their extraordinary ability. In fact, what is not perceived is that that individual has worked extraordinarily hard to develop their talent. It is just they completed that work in previous lives and have carried what they learned into this life via deep essence.

Why does one person work so hard to develop their abilities to a level at which they are seen to be displaying talent? Because it is their bliss to do so. This applies to every field of human endeavour. Those individuals who make extraordinary contributions to their field are not functioning at that level by luck, because their parents were talented in the same field (although they may well be), or because of a propitious conjunction of genes (although genetically inherited traits may have contributed to their make-up this time round). They operate at that extraordinarily high level because they have worked at it over a sequence of lives. Furthermore, they selected a genetically structured body, a family and a social environment to be born into this time round that would enable them to best give expression to their serially-developed talent. What, then, is responsible for genius?

THE MYTH OF GENIUS

Geniuses are abundantly talented people whose accomplishments are noticed by others, whether positively, such as the scientific genius of Albert

Einstein or Madam Curie, or negatively, the so-called evil genius of Adolph Hitler. In fact, genius is a term invented at the level of the socialised self in order to direct applause or approbation towards others. This is unnecessary because it merely generates another layer of social hierarchy, placing a few on a pedestal and the mass of humanity far below.

The truth is that talent is far from uncommon and is spread through all levels of human fields and interactions. It is just that most individual's talents are noticed by few others. There are the obvious examples of writers such as William Blake and Emily Dickinson whose talent remained largely unrecognised until after their deaths. Many people in quite ordinary occupations have a talent that is perceived only by those with whom they immediately interact. Their talent may be with managing children, managing adults, simplifying the complex and so making the difficult appear easy, or helping others appreciate that they are much more than how they feel. And so on.

In common parlance, talented people are often called gifted, as if some other being—in the past the expectation was God—had given that person their talent. We consider the use of the word "gifted" in relation to talent as inappropriate. Everyone works for what they possess and who they are. There is no chance. There is no gifting. Talent simply results from focused intent and extended application driven by a passion to realise one's bliss.

The final point we wish to make about growth for now is in relation to each individual's average thousand life trajectory.

CHAPTER 6

A Question of Trajectories

W HAT WE WILL ATTEMPT TO DESCRIBE IN THIS CHAPTER IS THE process by which a spiritual identity progresses through an extended series of lives. We term this serial multi-life progress a trajectory. To clarify what is intended by trajectory, envisage all possible human experiences as existing within a three-dimensional field. Each individual fragment of spiritual consciousness follows, or rather, establishes through personal choice, its unique trajectory through this three-dimensional space.

In normal circumstances, an object that traverses a three-dimensional space, such as a bullet, travels on the trajectory that is established for it when initial momentum is established. In the case of a bullet, this is when the gun is fired. The bullet then follows that trajectory, without deviating, until it is acted on by another force. Discounting gravity for the sake of discussion, let's say the bullet travels until it strikes and glances off an object. It is then deflected and begins to travel on a secondary trajectory. It follows this new trajectory either until all its energy dissipates or it strikes another object and its trajectory is altered a second time. However, each time it is deflected, the bullet begins to follow a new trajectory according to parameters established by its initial firing, which are adjusted by the subsequent impacts.

It may be said that a bullet only ever follows a trajectory established for it by other forces. The trajectory a spiritual identity takes through the manifold experiences offered by human life has many similarities to that of a bullet. That is what we will discuss in this chapter.

MOMENTUM AND ACCUMULATED HUMAN IDENTITY

When a spiritual identity begins its thousand life series of incarnations, it has a starting point and certain level of energy. The starting point is provided by the place in which it first incarnates. The energy is provided by the body into which it incarnates and by the innate drives and dispositions present in its core consciousness. Certain things happen to the identity during its initial incarnation, it reacts to what happens to it in particular ways, and this combination of outwardly sourced experiences and inward responses combine to generate a momentum.

The next life will likely start in a similar set of social circumstances as the first life, so the identity may develop familiarity with those specific conditions and draw on what it learned first time round. It then undergoes subsequent experiences, which the individual spirit responds to in turn. In this way psychospiritual momentum is developed and maintained.

It is usual that each spiritual identity repeats a particular set of social circumstances until its feels comfortable in those circumstances, coming to know what to expect and how to negotiate fruitfully within that social environment. Only once this is achieved, and it has gained basic interactive skills, does the identity then try exploring other kinds of social environments, which are perhaps a little more complex and so a little more demanding. In this way it takes baby steps, progressively learning as a baby does, all the time developing its motor, cognitive and social skills.

In these early incarnations a momentum is established that is fed by the chosen environments and by the individual's inner responses to those environments. As it accumulates lives, and extracts life lessons from each, its knowledge of how to negotiate human existence increases, and it becomes more confident within itself, entirely because, like a six year old child, it has started to develop a sense of accumulated personal human identity. This human identity develops a momentum of its own as the greater spiritual identity incarnates time after time.

It could be said that on the one hand this accumulated human identity is a limiting factor because once a psychological momentum is established, in a sense the spiritual identity is tied to that accumulated human identity—an identity, we must make clear, that is of its own making, because it develops as a result of its own human level reactions to human existence.

After several hundred lives, each incarnating spirit has developed a range of personally significant psychological traits. These traits, some quite contradictory to others, comprise the dominant psychological characteristics of the individual's accumulated human identity. However, they ultimately sheet back to the core dispositions fixed in the nature of each individual spiritual identity. This is because from the very first incarnation, and ever after, each individual's core disposition will incline one individual to respond in particular ways to life circumstances, while another individual, possessing a different set of traits related to its core disposition, will reaction differently to the same set of circumstances. As a result, the second individual develops its own accumulated human identity, similarly constituted of psychological characteristics that may be sheeted back to that individual's core disposition.

In a sense, core disposition may be viewed as providing an initial set of psychological parameters that function much as a gun imparts energy and momentum to a bullet. The bullet travels on a trajectory dictated by the initial conditions provided by the gun. Implicit in these initial conditions are direction, height, speed, and target. In the same way, a spiritual identity has the equivalents of direction, height, speed, and target. But these only begin to become apparent to the spirit itself as it experiences a sequence of lives. Let's begin unpicking this analogy with a consideration of target.

THE TARGET OF INCARNATION

Most human beings have no idea of what their multi-life target consists of. That is, they have no idea of what they are aiming to achieve by living life after life. Indeed, few people have a clear sense of what they are striving to achieve in this current incarnation. They may have a strong sense of what work, occupation, or passion drives them. But few understand what their purpose is in engaging in whatever they feel passionately drawn towards.

Previously, we have drawn attention to what the target is, both in terms of each individual life and in a series of lives. As a general statement, the target life by life is to have particular experiences from which one can draw life lessons. Of course, how this plays out in detail for each individual is complex. We have initiated the writing of this series of books precisely to illuminate what is involved. Overall, the target is to evolve as a spiritual fragment, and in so doing to achieve one's bliss.

No one achieves their bliss in each life. Some lives focus on developing skills that will be utilised in subsequent incarnations. Some lives are to repair impingements on others made during previous lives. Some lives are entirely designed to help others, mostly friends in spirit, develop their own skills and achieve their own goals. And some lives are pauses, designated periods when prior life lessons are absorbed and, in a sense, one takes a deep breath before beginning a new series of tasks. Nonetheless, the ultimate target towards which any spirit aims is that of realising its bliss within the human domain. This aim provides each spirit with the momentum that gives it a trajectory through the extensive multi-dimensional field that is human experience.

THE FOUR PHASES OF HUMAN TRAJECTORIES

Many experiences are available within the human domain. Some spirits taste many. Others taste fewer but enter into them more deeply. As in everyday life, some spirits are grasshoppers, jumping from experience to experience. Others are elephants, moving more slowly, but with great purpose. Yet others are like felines, slinking quietly, waiting for a propitious moment, then pouncing.

What dictates how an individual responds to the possibilities offered by human incarnation is in part innate disposition and in part reflects the outlook one develops as a result of repeated lives. This is where the comparison between the bullet's trajectory through the air and a spirit's trajectory through the possibilities provided by human existence breaks down. A bullet is only fired once and it only changes its trajectory if it strikes another object. In contrast, in a sense each new human incarnation is new firing, and a spirit may alter its own trajectory in mid-flight.

After sixty incarnations or so, the spirit begins to develop a sense of its own human identity and has also developed sufficient confidence in its ability to try new experiences. Prior to this it has focused on acquiring rudimentary skills and overcoming its fear of new experiences. To continue the animal analogy, the naïve spirit is like a field mouse, easily frightened, and careful not to attract attention, jumping back into the safe haven of its nest whenever its feels uncomfortable. After sixty or so incarnations it has matured sufficiently not to need a hole in the ground. It becomes more like a grasshopper, leaping from one experience to another.

The grasshopper phase is the part of the incarnation cycle when individuals sample a wide range of often unrelated experiences because they want to learn what experiences are available. Jumping around provides information for the next phase of their development. At the grasshopper stage spirits are also aware that there are predators in the human domain so, like grasshoppers in nature, they keep in groups. Essentially, where naïve spirits seek safety in a nest, slightly more experienced spirits seek safety in numbers.

During their grasshopper phase spirits find some experiences a fascinating fit, others they are largely indifferent to, yet others they know they must avoid in future—and, remember, individuals respond individually, so experiences that attract one individual repel another, and visa versa. Following their grasshopper phase, spirits start focusing on specific lines of experience. This is so they can acquire specific skills, which helps them develop abilities in fields of human activity to which they are attracted.

The third period may be metaphorically referred to as the feline period. Felines hunt either in small groups or alone. At this stage of their development individual spirits feel confident of their personal powers. They are happy to travel into unknown territories with just a few trusted friends in spirit. Or, if they feel confident enough, they even occasionally initiate a series of lives largely on their own, testing themselves in new terrain, sometimes friendly, at other times filled with enemies—and we speak metaphorically, not literally, enemies in this sense being individuals who are focused on their own goals and so will bulldoze through any who get in their way, or else are simply not inclined to lend a helping hand.

To return to our feline metaphor, this is a phase during which spirits, like stalking cats, weigh up the possibilities, think through impacts, and only then jump into a new experience. By now they have lived hundreds of lives and so have a considerable store of prior experience to draw on. They also know what they want to develop within themselves. Hence they very carefully choose their upcoming lives and what they wish to work through, confront and achieve in each life. Where the field mouse timorously jumps back into its protective hole, and where the grasshopper blithely leaps from juicy-looking shoot to juicy-looking shoot, the feline conserves its energy and only leaps when it has a considered purpose in mind.

These three levels of development reflect the kinds of trajectories individuals take through the field of all possible human experiences. Spirits are timorous at first and tend to keep to a narrow band of experiences. After they develop skills and gain confidence they have a period of jumping from experience to experience, sometimes making wild leaps. After a trial period of tasting different aspects of human existence they settle down, identifying bands of experiences they wish to explore in greater depth. They then enter their feline phase, making deliberate leaps from one field of experience to another, all with the aim of accumulating specific life lessons, developing particular abilities, and using the chosen opportunities to express their bliss. Finally, they enter the elephant stage, in which there is no leaping. This is the last phase of incarnation, when what has been learning and developed is consolidated and any unresolved prior life issues are tidied up.

As usual we add several riders to our metaphor. First, this is not meant to provide a definitive developmental scale of any sort. This is no more than an attempt to indicate, in simple terms, what is much more complex in reality. It is offered as a taste of how spirits establish a trajectory for themselves through the many possibilities offered by incarnation.

We also observe that some spirits have an elephant approach to their incarnations from day one. That is, they quickly establish a trajectory, and they follow it tenaciously, deviating little. Other spirits have a touch of mouse or grasshopper to their natures, being timorous or jumping often, tasting widely but at no great depth. For some, these kind of trajectories result from innate disposition. For example, an individual with a dominant percentage of the introspective modality may not jump much at all throughout their trajectory, moving steadily on a clear line. Others with a warrior disposition and a dominant expressive modularity may be quite fearless and jump into the unlikeliest situations. For others, being a mouse, grasshopper, feline or elephant is almost entirely a matter of choice. As we keep repeating, the possibilities are extensive, and when a naïve spirit incarnates for its very first human life nothing is set in stone.

The upshot of all this is that if one made a graph of, say, one million spirits as they propelled themselves through their series of an average of one thousand lives, at first there would be small steps, then there would be larger jumps in a variety of directions but collectively gradually moving forwards. Next there would be an orchestrated series of jumps that while moving forwards also kept returning to similar places but further along the developmental curve. This phase of the overall trajectory would appear quite patterned due to a restricted range of experiences being returned to repeatedly, but with each repetition involving a deeper level of experience and progressively greater levels of ability, all designed to achieve mastery in self-selected fields of endeavour. Right at the end of the trajectory it straightens. The trajectory ends when much has been experienced and learned, and the spirit has achieved sufficient levels of love and knowledge that it is now ready to move onto the next phase of its evolution.

What we previously discussed regarding spirits choosing to make a significant departure from their prior trajectory most usually occurs during the grasshopper and feline phases. This is when experimentation is carried out. It is also when spirits are most likely to feel that they want to do things completely differently. Of course, significant departures can occur as early as the mouse phase, particularly in the case of individual fragments who are innately adventurous or who, for whatever reason, are not daunted by consequences. Significant departures from the overall multi-life trajectory at what we have termed the elephant phase are highly unlikely, given that this phase is not about new experiences but about bringing the entire series of incarnations to its developmental close.

However, sometimes individuals choose to make a significant deviation from the trajectory they themselves have planned, very possibly for several lives. At such times they deliberately go off plan.

THE CLOAK OF INSCRUTABILITY

Human personality is a complex construct. As we have been at pains to point out, some of the traits that contribute to personality are genetically inherited, others are socially conditioned, and others are brought in from previous lives. Deep preferences and passions emanating from the spiritual core disposition psychologically push individuals in certain directions rather than others. Furthermore, choice is always available, adding an unexpected element that, in effect, throws a cloak of inscrutability over the entire psychospiritual edifice. In using the phrase "cloak of inscrutability", what we mean is that because nothing in human existence is cast in stone, no outcome is ever certain and finalised before it occurs. Accordingly, no one—and we include non-embodied observers and helpers in this—can ever know all that a person will do during and with the circumstances they have planned for a life.

In general, an individual's psychological make-up, along with their pre-selected life goal, will push them in a particular direction, and within that direction they are *more likely* to make certain choices than others. However, at any time individuals can rise above the inclinations of their own psychological make-up and make a choice none previously foresaw as likely.

How is this possible? Because, at their core, human beings are spiritual identities. And no spiritual identity is bound by the limitations of the human everyday awareness and its associated human identity that it has chosen this time round. Other choices can be made at any time, no matter how far plans are advanced. The surprising choices individuals sometimes make generates unpredictability. This means that no one can completely predict how a life will turn out. There are odds, of course, as we have just observed. Given any extended population, it is the norm that the majority will act in conformity with their own pre-life choices. But there are always a number who depart from the norm, sometimes to a degree of magnitudes.

Indeed, to some extent behaviour that departs from the norm is inevitable, given that each individual incarnates an average of one thousand times. During that number of incarnations almost everyone, at some time, throws their hands in the air (metaphorically speaking, of course), and says to themselves, "You know what? I'm going off plan right now!"

THE PLEASURES AND RISKS OF GOING OFF PLAN

There are many reasons why people choose to depart from their life plan. The motive may be frustration, or a desire to have fun, or plain being bored with repetition. The decision to go off plan may result from a sense of mischievousness, arise out of exasperation with having made so many safe choices, or simply reflect dissatisfaction with personal tentativeness. Whatever the motive, the result is a substantial departure from the overall trajectory that they have already established.

Such departures must not be viewed as errors of judgement. In fact, they often provide momentous turning points in a sequence of incarnations. A substantial departure from a well established multi-incarnation trajectory can greatly enhance a particular life, extending what was planned in radical—and personally pleasing—ways. At other times the departure can have catastrophic results for an individual and for everyone he or she is closely involved with.

Of course, even a catastrophic result is not necessarily a bad thing. Its most providential outcome is that it opens up entirely new avenues of possibilities, possibilities that the spiritual identity never previously thought it would find interesting or be able to cope with. Alternatively, it may close down, once and for all, a particular path of possibilities for growth that an individual had been pursuing for several lives. By jumping ahead in a series of possibilities, by tasting where the trajectory they have chosen is leading, individuals are put into an extreme situation that leads them to realise that, actually, that line of experience is not for them after all. Thus they come to appreciate that a line of growth that they have initiated, thinking it would be productive, is in fact not a satisfying fit with their core disposition. Without this radical divergence from their established trajectory, and particularly without its catastrophic outcome, they would have spent many more lives moving tentatively forwards before finally reaching the same conclusion: that they are travelling on a road that for them is a dead end.

As would be expected, deciding to depart from one's life plan while in the middle of living that life can be extremely disconcerting to others who are sharing the life. Those others will likely argue among themselves and with the individual making the decision, saying that he or she is doing the wrong thing, that the decision is going to disadvantage them in life, or that it is simply contrary to common sense. Some will fear that the individual is courting failure, even catastrophic failure. Yet for the individual concerned, departing radically from the life plan results in a wonderful life lesson, a lesson that would not have been as powerful or as profound if the original life plan was rigidly adhered to and faithfully carried out.

RADICAL DEPARTURES FROM THE LIFE TRAJECTORY

Of course, the mistake made by those viewing such an individual's radical life choice is that they are limited to a single life scenario, in which personal happiness and satisfaction must be achieved in just this lifetime. In contrast, we are considering these matters within a thousand life scenario averaged over an incarnating population of billions. In this much wider context, human beings taste, swallow, digest, and excrete numerous and diverse experiences—given that what is "digested" consists of experiences that the individual finds nutritious and that add to the stock of valuable life lessons, and what is "excreted" is a realisation that certain experiences do not fit satisfyingly with the aim of evolving one's innate nature and actually limit the achieving of one's goals.

The point we are making, in fact reiterating because we have stated it elsewhere on many occasions, is that a life can never be assessed as successful or unsuccessful in the context of everyday human existence, within the arc that extends from birth to death. The applause or approbation of other human beings when they respond to anyone else's life choices, and the apparently positive or negative life outcomes that result, is generally quite irrelevant when, after death, a spiritual identity looks back at the life just lived and extracts useful lessons from it.

An exception to this last statement is when, in fact, one of the goals for that life was precisely to gain the applause or approbation of others. In this single instance, others' approval or disapproval is significant. In reality, a much more common goal in relation to others' applause and approbation is learning to rise above other's projections. This is because, for the vast majority of individuals, much more in human everyday existence acts to keep them from realising their self-selected life tasks and goals than assists in their achievement.

To reiterate: The degree to which one fulfils or does not fulfil one's pre-selected life plan and its associated tasks and goals cannot be used to measure the success or failure of a particular life.

As we have stated elsewhere, and repeated in the above discussion regarding catastrophic departures from the life plan, individuals learn as much from their failures as from their successes. In the laboratory that is provided by human existence on this planet, everything that occurs—whether planned or not, whether chosen after much thought or dived into on the spur of the moment, whether one is diverted by accident, or whether others' choices impact unexpectedly on one's own plans—it all contributes to the life journey via which one experiences, learns and grows. Everything adds to the experiment that is a single human life. Everything contributes to the sought outcome, which is growth.

Having made these comments in order to elucidate the issue of trajectory through lives, we now progress to the theme of true personality.

PART THREE

THE NATURE OF
TRUE PERSONALITY

CHAPTER 7

What Constitutes
True Personality

TRUE PERSONALITY IS AN EXPRESSION OF THE INDIVIDUAL SPIRIT within a human personality, that personality being you this time round. Many factors have contributed to the shaping of your current personality. Behind them all is the disposition of your core spiritual self. This is the ongoing unique spiritual nature that is fundamental to who you are. It provides the engine that drives you forward from one incarnation to the next. It has chosen your current personality.

To incarnate, a spirit requires just two things: a body and an associated personality. Each is a complex organic mechanism. Over the course of its full incarnational cycle a spirit will "wear" approximately one thousand personalities. Each personality, technically each *sub*-personality, is a unique combination of psychological traits, although sometimes the differences between personalities is subtle.

Each personality is selected by you to help you achieve specific outcomes. As we noted earlier, outcomes become more complex the more a spirit incarnates. An inexperienced spirit has fewer potential outcomes to select from because it possesses fewer skills and so can take on less. As the spirit accumulates a stock of experiences, acquires skills, and comes to appreciate how to best use its periods of immersion in the human domain, potential outcomes become progressively more focused and the sub-personalities selected to facilitate the realisation of those outcomes become ever more nuanced. Two important points can be made with respect to this process.

DEVELOPING PSYCHOSPIRITUAL MOMENTUM

As a spirit progresses through the trajectory of its lives, it develops individual momentum. This results from the spirit coming to appreciate what works best for it in the human domain. What works best is learned through trial and error. Some spirits latch onto what works for them quickly. For others it takes much longer. Some spirits are naturally more conservative and play it safer in their selection, while others like to stretch themselves via the sub-personalities they select, perhaps even to breaking point—of the sub-personality and not of the spirit, of course.

However the spirit comes to appreciate what works best for it, and whether that appreciation comes earlier or later, the result is that the spirit accumulates preferred ways of functioning in the human domain. This results in a particular psychospiritual momentum. A significant contributor to that momentum is what in the previous chapter we called accumulated human identity.

ACCUMULATED HUMAN IDENTITY

Accumulated human identity comprises all the character traits a spirit has "tried on for size" throughout the totality of its lives. Some traits are found conducive to growth, or are just plain fun to manifest and so are fostered, while others the spirit does not find useful or enjoyable and chooses not to continue working with. Some personality traits lead to benevolent behaviour, while others create problems for the individual and those with whom it interacts. These latter are the useful obstacle traits we have previously discussed.

The traits of accumulated human identity are grounded in the experiences of the biological self, the socialised self and the essence self, and are stored as deep essence traits. These deep essence traits are themselves part of an even larger store of experiential material, which includes: experiences resulting from choices made, neglected or rejected; repeated behaviours, changed behaviours, repeated reactions to others' behaviours; successes, mistakes and lessons learned; and skills, abilities and talents developed in the many different fields of human activity. There is also a store of karma, a store of obligations (which results from as yet unfulfilled promises made to reciprocate help the spirit has received), and a store of goodwill. This last incorporates the largess of compassion, benevolence, and love that the spirit naturally shares in its non-embodied state but that it has to learn to share in the human domain.

Listed baldly in this way, it is a daunting store of experiential material. It indicates why, as experience accrues from hundreds of incarnations, choosing the components of future lives becomes ever more complex. This is a major reason why the late teen and adult phases of incarnation are so difficult. Much experience has been accumulated, but the spirit has not yet learned how to juggle its deep essence stores, its long-term aims, its karmic responsibilities, its obligations, and its desire to share, with the daily pleasant and trying situations basic to human existence, and its own often inappropriate responses to those situations, which lead to transgressions that then need to be addressed in later lives. All these factors contribute to the shaping of each individual's accumulated human identity, and need to be taken into account when a new life plan is being formulated.

TRANSGRESSIONS, FINE-TUNING, RESPONSIBILITIES

With regard to transgressions, there is a common saying that time is a healer. For human beings, time involves repetition. Repetition in itself doesn't heal, but it does provide opportunities for individuals to integrate all the material they accumulate in the experientially rich human realm. It is by integrating disparate and often contradictory experiences that healing occurs.

The process of integrating diverse materials may be likened to the process of cooking, in which dry ingredients are shaken through a sieve. The sieve holds back lumps, allowing through only the finely sifted ingredients, which are then mixed in the bowl. The same process occurs on the psychological level. The repeated "wearing" of diverse psychological traits results in them being progressively "shaken" into a refined state, then sieved and captured in a "bowl," which is the spiritual individual's store of accumulated deep essence traits.

Accordingly, each sub-personality is a work in progress, generated by the spirit as it works to refine the psychological make-up of its still accumulating human identity. Fine-tuning is required to get any sub-personality's traits functioning at an optimal level. The way fine-tuning takes place is that the traits being worked on are adopted in a series of sub-personalities. The combinations of traits are varied subtly from one life to the next as the spirit strives to refine the balance between the traits it is working on. This is the sifting process, using the conditions of human life to purify and develop traits. Fine-tuning continues until the spirit decides the traits are functioning optimally. Then another set of traits are selected and the same process begins again.

Each sub-personality is a work-in-progress in another sense. A single sub-personality is one step in a putative thousand towards the spiritual identity's final integration of all it experiences, develops and learns. But growth is not just inwardly focused. It also involves other individuals.

Children can have carefree lives because they don't have adult responsibilities weighing them down. Similarly, inexperienced spirits live freer lives and have fewer responsibilities than more experienced spirits—because they have fewer skills and so cannot take on as much. As a result, immature spirits also have fewer choices. It is only as spirits build an experiential store and develop their abilities that more possibilities become available to them. The irony is that with more possibilities also goes greater responsibility. And taking responsibility narrows choice. We'll explain.

Clearly, as a spirit's knowhow increases, more choices open up to it. But spirits, while "wearing" a sub-personality, choose poorly as well as well. So all inevitably transgress against others at some time. Transgressions need to be addressed. When a spirit chooses to address a transgression, other attractive possibilities must be set aside. In effect, options are reduced. However—and here we draw attention to yet another irony—while taking on responsibilities reduces immediate options, it simultaneously initiates more subtle interactions. These in turn lead to more nuanced experiences, which facilitate further psychological growth. With the individual now possessing greater maturity, new possibilities become available that haven't been available previously.

So taking on responsibilities reduces immediate options, but in the long-term it leads to the availability of previously unavailable options. Like everything else in the human domain, responsibly addressing transgressions involves trade-offs. But the trade-offs help fine-tune your accumulated human identity. This is the first point regarding the constitution of your true personality this time round: it is a sub-personality that possesses traits specifically chosen by you to enhance the growth of your greatest current work in progress, your own accumulated human identity.

The second point has to do with how true personality's constituent parts interact to contribute to your journey through this life.

LAUNCHING TRUE PERSONALITY

It will be understood by now that your current sub-personality may be viewed as consisting of both true personality and false personality. False personality is centred in the socialised self, true personality in the essence self. True personality is made up of several psychological components. The relationship of these components may be best appreciated via a metaphor.

Picture a boat motoring across the sea of human experience. The boat is your essence self. The boat's engine is your spiritual self. It's the engine because it drives your existence this time round. It decided the when and where of the journey your boat is on in this life. It has also selected the boat's essential components: your life plan, life goal, type, orientation and attitude.

You, at the level of your spiritual identity, have prepared a significant journey for this boat. Your life plan represents your planned voyage. It includes particular ports of call, people you have agreed to meet at those ports, and other boats you wish to connect up with. Some boats you plan to travel with in large or small flotillas. Others you will dock beside for a short time only, share information or experiences, then leave behind. While your boat may or may not end up following the course plotted by your life plan, each boat at its launch—that is, each individual at birth—has a pre-mapped voyage.

The life goal is the boat's ballast. It provides a sense of satisfaction, affirming to you that your voyage is progressing as planned. (The seven life goals are growth, re-evaluation, dominance, submission, acceptance, rejection and equilibrium. They are discussed in *Practical Spirituality*.) An important function of the life goal is to prevent the boat from tipping over. When times get tough, the captain, who is your spiritual self, uses the life goal to bring the boat back onto an even keel. Of course, some boats over-balance and sink. While sinking before the full voyage has been sailed is viewed as a catastrophe on the human level, on the spiritual level sinking is okay because going under is another learning experience. And when death ensues, it is only that sub-personality and its body that dies. The spiritual identity carries on. To rework a common saying, it lives to float another day.

Orientation is the rudder. It steers the essence self through the rough, choppy, and calm waters of human interactions. Where the life goal functions as ballast, rebalancing the boat when it tips too far to one side or the other, orientation brings the boat back on course. In this sense, the two work in tandem. The difference between them is that the life goal steadies the boat as the engine of the spiritual self drives it on, while orientation re-points the boat in the chosen direction when it is blown off-course. Psychologically, orientation manifests as one of seven traits: power, caution, passion, repression, aggression, perseverance, and observation. They will be discussed in the next chapter.

Attitude is the prow of the boat. It slices through the waters of human experience. When you journey towards other people, what they see first is the prow of your boat coming towards them. In contrast, your boat's rudder and ballast are under water so remain invisible. Similarly, attitude is visible to those who wish to look, while life goal and orientation are psychologically hidden from view. Another way of saying this is that the psychological traits of life goal and orientation are buried in the essence self, while attitude overflows from the essence self into the socialised self. Given that initial interactions between people tend to occur at the level of their socialised selves, attitude is the essence trait most easily observed by others. Only as people come to know each other do the buried traits of life goal and orientation become visible—but, again, only if people look for them. There are seven attitudes in all. They will be discussed shortly.

The final key essence characteristic is type. Type may be likened to the boat's communication system. It is how you receive, process, and share information. There are three dominant essence types, moving, emotional and intellectual. Each of these is further divided into moving, emotional or intellectual, generating a total of nine primary sub-categories of type.

The intention behind this metaphor of comparing the essence self to a boat is to present concepts that may seem somewhat programmatic, even mechanical—given life plan, orientation, and attitude each come in seven varieties, and type in nine—and situate them into a wider context in which choice, options and responsibilities are always in play.

Existence is organic, not mechanical. No outcomes are set. No rules dictate how lives play out. Nonetheless, within the organic interplay of multiple factors it is useful to divide human reality into smaller bite-sized concepts, entirely to more clearly perceive what is going on. This is why we are now embarking on a discussion of the fourteen essence traits of orientation and attitude. The divisions may appear schematic, but they are useful to understanding what you are doing in your life this time round, and particularly *how* you are doing it psychologically.

CHAPTER 8

Orienting Your Life

ORIENTATION PROVIDES A PSYCHOLOGICAL MEANS TO NEGOTIATE tricky life circumstances. When individuals become so caught up in daily living that they lose connection with their spiritual self's drive to learn and grow, orientation steers the individual back onto task. Simply, orientation is an essence level psychological trait an individual uses to help them steer through problems and accomplish their life plan.

Drawing on the framework offered by the Michael Teachings, we identify seven basic essence level orientations. These consist of the self-actualising pair of aggression and perseverance, the self-transforming pair of passion and repression, the self-fulfilling pair of power and caution, and self-neutralising observation. We will briefly discuss each, place it within the incarnational cycle, and comment on pairing.

CAUTION

We start with caution because it is one of the two most common orientations. It manifests most visibly in cautious behaviour. People are cautious in all kinds of ways. They are commonly cautious when interacting with others, especially those they don't know well. They are cautious when making big life decisions. They are doubly cautious when deciding who to share intimate confessions with. And they are extremely cautious when choosing who to expose their most deeply felt emotions to.

We note that caution in the way we are discussing it here is not driven by fear. It simply results in individuals being cautious in their choices and the way they process life circumstances. Being cautious is an entirely reasonable response to human life conditions. People are complex, have concealed agendas and motives, and it is difficult to gauge another's intent. This is especially so in today's cities where people can live quite anonymously and relatively easily pretend they are other than they actually are. This is in contrast to life in small towns and villages, where many people may be related, or people have grown up together. Here caution is not required as a default because others' characters are well known. It is because so many people are living in cities today that caution has become the most common orientation—although we note that in practice anyone living anywhere can have a caution orientation.

Of course, there is a problem with being overly cautious. An individual may be so cautious that opportunities are missed, to the individual's disadvantage. Why then is caution so often chosen? It is chosen because individuals feel they need to carefully appraise opportunities before acting. It may be that in prior lives they have been intemperate and spontaneously made

THE SEVEN ORIENTATIONS

	(+)	(−)
SELF-ACTUALISING		
AGGRESSION	Dynamism	Belligerence
PERSEVERANCE	Persistence	Immutability
SELF-TRANSFORMING		
POWER	Authority	Oppression
CAUTION	Deliberation	Procrastination
SELF-FULFILLING		
PASSION	Self-actualisation	Identification
REPRESSION	Restraint	Inhibition
SELF-NEUTRALISING		
OBSERVATION	Clarity	Surveillance

decisions that disadvantaged them. Accordingly, they now want to learn how to hold back and deliberate on options before making decisions.

Alternatively, they may have overcompensated in previous lives, withdrawing from active engagement to survive in environments they felt were too harsh, demanding or dangerous. After having been withdrawn for several lives they are now learning to re-engage with the rough and tumble of human life. But they want to re-engage gradually. Being cautious is a way to do that, putting out feelers like a snail does. When the snail feels threatened it withdraws into its shell. After the threat has passed it re-emerges and puts out its feelers again, testing the environment to check it is safe before fully emerging and carrying on. Individuals who have had difficult previous lives may select the caution orientation to act as a snail does, being cautious to reduce the feeling of being overwhelmed.

To translate this into developmental terms, a young child may be energetic and boisterous, testing others' limits and getting into all kinds of scrapes. This often happens during the period parents call the terrible twos, when children start developing a sense of identity. However, when the child starts interacting with others, who may be even more boisterous than it is, it can get into trouble. It learns a lesson in the kindergarten of hard knocks that it needs to be more careful in its social interactions. Thus it learns to be cautious.

In the same way, as an incarnating spirit enters the childhood phase of its incarnation cycle it often becomes cautious, reflective of the fact that during previous lives it experienced the rough and tumble of life, over which it had no control. It now wishes to learn control. One way to achieve this is to become more considered in its decision-making, so it doesn't end up walking into environments that are physically or emotionally overwhelming. It also needs to learn to keep its responses to threats under control.

Caution has been adopted by so many people because so many are currently passing through this phase. Their choice of caution is reinforced by the fact that many human social environments are complex and difficult. Coercion and hostility are commonplace. So caution is an entirely natural and understandable choice. Caution helps individual spirits undergo diverse human experiences without being overwhelmed. In a psychological sense, caution creates a pause between information entering the everyday aware-

ness and the individual responding to the information. Reacting instanta-
neously is what gets people into trouble. Caution puts a break on reactions
by pushing the individual to reflect before acting.

This has several outcomes. It gives the individual time to deliberate. It
stops the individual stepping into trouble. And it prevents new karma being generated. It especially helps to generate a new, more mature way of responding to difficult situations, creating a new pattern of behaviour. In this
way caution facilitates self-transformation.

Caution may be adopted at any time during the incarnation cycle.
Naïve spirits are understandably cautious in a world that is new to them,
where they are struggling to develop the skills to cope. During the grasshopper phase spirits tend to have more confidence and so may be less cautious as
they hop between experiential possibilities. Yet they do tend to keep in large
groups, so their explorations occur within the context of what they view as
safe environments. Once a spirit becomes more experienced, and especially
after coming up against others who are exploitative or oppressive, it may re-
vert to being cautious for a time. This often occurs during the feline phase,
when spirits more carefully weigh up their options before leaping. During the
final elephant phase spirits may adopt a cautious orientation simply because
they have experienced much of the worst—and the best—of human existence,
and now simply wish to keep a low profile while they resolve outstanding issues and bring their final tasks and aims to a satisfactory conclusion.

As a final note, we observe that the caution orientation does not automatically result in passive behaviour. Many individuals, especially earlier
in their incarnation cycle, use violence to control their environment, lashing
out when they feel threatened—which, for those in the timorous field mouse
phase, can be often. As these individuals become more experienced they
learn to use violence judiciously to fulfil their desires. Yet throughout they
are, in fact, being cautious. Their caution manifests in the way they stick to
social environments they are familiar with and do not challenge themselves
with new experiences or ways of living. This indicates how the caution orientation may lead to individuals achieving little and being slow to develop.
Only after repeated incarnations do these individuals gain confidence, shake
off safety offered by caution, and start taking larger developmental steps.

POWER

Caution is paired with the orientation of power. Power manifests behaviourally in being authoritative. Where those functioning in the caution orientation seek to develop control in their social environment by weighing things up before acting, those functioning in the power mode seek to control their environment, and others in it, by having mastery over them.

Like everything else in life, authoritativeness can be applied to life situations crudely or subtly, mechanically or with mastery. For those with a power orientation the social roles of policeman and bureaucrat offer an opportunity to apply rules and laws. They can perform their socially sanctioned roles crudely, through mechanical application and dogged bullying, or with understanding and finesse. How they apply power is itself influenced by the sub-personality's other traits. For example, if the policeman or bureaucrat has a life goal of dominance, that will reinforce their power orientation and likely make them absolute terrors. Life experience—more exactly, multi-life experience—is also significant, because when individuals have been on the receiving end of crudely applied power they are more likely to appreciate the harm it can do.

As individuals mature, rather than bluntly wielding authority, they may seek authority within a specific field of human endeavour. They do so by becoming masterful in that field. Rather than being dominant socially, their dominance derives from developed expertise. For the mature, the power orientation drives them through their life, urging them on to new achievements. It may also ensure they are never entirely satisfied with what they have done, because they can always have greater knowledge and expertise. For this reason, the power orientation is useful for those with a life goal of growth.

Developmentally, the power orientation can be adopted at any time throughout the incarnational cycle. In the early phases it is usually applied somewhat bluntly, as just noted. The power orientation comes into its own during the mature phases, when individuals have a specific set of aims and tasks to fulfil, and select power as their orientation because it provides focus and steers their efforts in attaining them. Power in this sense is instrumental to self-transformation, facilitating learning and growing.

The downside is that individuals can become so caught up in achieving their own goals that they trample over others, especially others who are more delicate, more cautious, or who are simply less experienced and so need nurturing to help them get through life. Those possessing the power orientation often simply breeze past—or over the top of—such people, too impatient to give them the attention they require so they may fulfil their own tasks. So where those with a caution orientation limit themselves through being over-timid, but on the other hand do not impinge on others either and so do not tend to accrue karmic baggage, those with a power orientation can get a lot done, but if they are insensitive in the way they do it, and especially if they slip into negative, domineering behaviours, they may accrue considerable karmic baggage that will have to be worked through in subsequent lives—perhaps through adopting caution.

This brings us to the idea that orientations are paired. It may be thought that caution is somewhat more introspective while power is outwardly directed. They must not be viewed so simplistically, given the reverse can equally apply. Caution is frequently outwardly directed, which occurs when an individual gets others to carefully consider what they are doing before they act, as is done by environmental activist groups. Power becomes inwardly focused when it is applied to a field of personal development over which the individual wishes to gain personal mastery.

In practice, caution manifests as hesitation, power manifests in powering ahead. Having the ability to utilise either orientation at the appropriate time—hesitating in order to carefully consider, then acting with mastery—is an extremely useful skill. But when individuals carefully consider too much, and end up procrastinating, or when they overreact without any thought whatsoever, the result is painfully slow on the first hand and messy on the second. Immature individuals are locked into one extreme. Mature individuals have developed the psychological ability to pause and think things through when appropriate, and also to act decisively when that is required.

What all this shows is that these two orientations are paired because they are the extreme variations of a single orientation. In order to learn how to apply paired orientations appropriately, individuals usually adopt each extreme for several lives, using first one then the other in a range of life situations in order to become able to apply them in a balanced manner. The goal is to use either one, or both together, as appropriate.

Maturity manifests as flexibility. In human interactions one size never fits all. Neither is it appropriate to use one particular orientation to address each and every life situation. Multiple psychological approaches and abilities are required. Developing a mature level of flexibility requires individuals to build up a serious depth of experiential stock on which they can draw. Such stock is only developed through trial and error. There is no way to sculpt subtle psychological abilities except by jumping in, trying on various personality traits for size, refining them through trial and error, and ultimately finding out which do and do not work for you.

PASSION

At first glance, those with an orientation of passion appear to others as a flamboyant, get-it-out-there characters, sparkling, spontaneous, and quick to take up any opportunity to participate in what is happening. Passion people love to live life to the fullest. Those who have a caution orientation often look at such people enviously, wishing they could be so spontaneous and free. Naturally, while there is some truth in these observations, the passion orientation is more complex than this.

Simply, the passion orientation is adopted by those who wish to intensify their life experiences to generate powerful life lessons. Of course, those who possess the passion orientation may not realise this is what they are doing, especially if they remain unaware of their life plan. This lack of self-knowledge results in many people with a passion orientation throwing themselves into all kinds of experiences with great energy and intensity, but without realising that in the long term some situations are actually of far greater significance to them than others. The significant situations are those engineered to facilitate life lessons. The urge to engage passionately in significant situations comes from the spiritual self. The passion orientation intensifies the engineered situations, making the experience vivid and intensely engaging. This all helps the individual work through pre-selected issues. We will give an example.

Imagine an individual has been oppressed in a prior life. Typical examples are social oppression, such as being a servant, serf or slave who is treated inhumanely, being sexually exploited, or being discriminated against on the basis of skin colour, social status, age, sex, or how much money one doesn't have. When oppression, exploitation or discrimination is sustained over the course of a life a powerful psychological impression is made at the essence level. This occurs whether one is a perpetrator or a recipient. The powerful psychological impression, along with whatever karmic debts and obligations have been stockpiled, then becomes part of the individual spirit's accumulated human identity. In a subsequent life, the spirit creates a life plan to address the negative aspects of the psychological impressions. The spirit may commit to taking up the fight against whatever form of oppression, exploitation, or discrimination it participated in previously. Not only does this mean re-engaging with the same situation, it also involves meeting up with others who were previously caught up in the very same situation and who now also want to address the psychological limitations generated, redress karmic debts, and fulfil obligations to others to help them resolve their issues.

The passion orientation helps all these individuals experience the new life situation with great intensity. As a result the sought life lessons hit home with real punch. If those spirits had selected the orientation of caution they wouldn't have been able to thrown itself into the new life situation with the same intensity, and definitely would not have felt slighted, ignored, frustrated, powerless, or empowered to anywhere near the same degree. This is why those with the passion orientation keenly feel "the whips and scorn" of the world, even when others view the situation and consider the lash to be light. Note two further points in relation to this.

After a life is complete, the spirit reviews what it did during that life. It decides, for example, that exploiting or oppressing others, as it had just done, is not a loving way to behave. To drive the lesson home experientially, it may decide to take on a role of being oppressed, or exploited or discriminated against. Alternatively, the spirit may decide it has learned all it can playing a recipient role and it now needs to work to make others aware of what they are doing, whether as perpetrator or recipient. So it decides to take on the role of social worker, lawyer, teacher, or social activist. Alternatively, a family or community situation may be organised, involving a number of spirits who wish to engage with the same issue from differing perspectives, which will facilitate their individual learning goals. Ultimately, what is important is not so much the particular role as the lesson that is learnt from the experience. This means that roles are selected not on the simple basis that one was on one end of the oppression equation in one life so has to be on the other end in the next. Rather, roles are selected on the basis of what will best facilitate the desired life lesson.

On the other hand, it *is* the case that performing one extremity of behaviour often triggers a move to experiencing the other extremity. So after being immersed in the behaviour of perpetrator a spirit will likely shift to playing a victim role. This way it learns what impact its prior behaviour had on others. When that lesson is absorbed it will likely later shift to an overview role in which it works against the behaviour's occurrence. Swinging from one extremity to the other, from being a perpetrator to learning how recipients feel, from feeling a victim to empowering oneself by enlightening others to what is going on, are necessary phases of learning life lessons. The lesson is learned when one achieves an overview.

Most individuals who are passionately engaged in social issues in this life are working through experiences of injustice undergone in previous lives. Those who fight sex exploitation, who are feminists or unionists, and who wish to right a particular social or economic wrong, are doing so because they were immersed in such activities in prior lives, experienced the debilitating impact involved, and now wish to help others rise out of such negative situations. What differentiates those with a passion orientation from everyone else is the intensity with which they throw themselves into such work.

An obvious problem presents itself at this point. Sometimes individuals are so passionately immersed in their work that they become unbalanced. Passion-driven activism may spill over into one-eyed intolerance, foulmouthed virulence, even injurious violence. The unionist who is against all bosses, the feminist who is against all men, the religionist who is against all who do not believe what he or she believes, have an unbalanced orientation. The underlying intent to do social good has mutated into extreme behaviour that leads to the perpetration of more wrongs. Over-compensating is a very common behaviour, for example when the desire to save unborn babies results in killing a doctor. A life lesson certainly results, but not the lesson that was sought.

The way passion manifests within a sub-personality is modified by the individual's experiential stocks. As a result, the passion orientation is expressed differently during the phases of an individual's overall incarnational cycle. In the initial mouse phase passion is rarely adopted. This is because passion intensifies experiences and spirits with only a few lives of experience under their belt struggle to cope with human existence as it is. They lack the psychological strength to sustain the passion orientation without going off the rails. Passion is more likely to be adopted after the spirit reaches the grasshopper stage. During this phase passion adds energy to experiences, but because engagement is still quite shallow the intensity itself remains relatively superficial.

It is during the feline phase, when spirits are working to bed in life lessons and enhance essence growth, that the passion orientation is most commonly adopted. By this phase not only does the spirit have the experiential stock to keep passion in balance with other traits, the spirit is also psychologically in a position to extract much of value from its intensified experiences.

During the elephant phase, when final lessons are being bedded in and outstanding karma and relationship issues resolved, passion is used more sparingly. Sometimes, such as when a spirit adopts the role of epicure or art maker or art lover, passion will be adopted to intensify sensual, emotional and erotic experiences. Those nearing the end of their cycle do tend to enjoy the pure distillation of experience that passion facilitates, given they no longer flail around under the passion spell like those in the earlier phases of their cycle, and given they are able to focus their intent with great precision. But in general those in the elephant phase prefer other subtler kinds of stimulus besides the outright passionate.

As we said, the passion orientation helps intensify experiences so spirits may extract significant life lessons. In this sense, passion sustains a bridge between chosen life situations and inner goals. Where caution and power are more general in their scope, passion intensifies specific experiences to promote inner growth. In this way it balances the outer and the inner. The other balancing orientation is repression.

REPRESSION

An orientation of repression is adopted when extreme measures are called for, when a spirit has to generate a radical intervention in the behaviour of their accumulated human identity. The repression orientation hinges on restraining oneself from becoming engaged with life situations. It is more extreme than caution, which is oriented towards weighing things up before choosing. The repression orientation is about holding oneself back from choosing.

Living a life of restraint is a difficult experience. Socially, it may manifest in the life of a nun or monk who live a cloistered existence. It may also be pursued in the country or in a small village, where one experiences little variation in one's yearly life cycle. The orientation of repression must not be confused with behaviour in which you repress others or others repress you. That kind of repression has to do with external forces oppressing individuals and limiting their life choices. In the repression orientation you are holding yourself back.

Why do so? Why does anyone need to adopt this extreme orientation? After all, isn't life about experiencing, processing, and learning? How can anyone do so if they are holding themselves back from experiencing? This is where the remedial function of repression comes into play.

There are occasions through their incarnation cycle when individuals get carried away. It may be that they do so very intensely during just one life. But usually getting carried away is a tendency that builds over a number of lives. Whether one gets carried away in many lives or just in one, the result is that a tendency becomes embedded as a deep essence trait.

Examples of such tendencies include excessive indulgence in guilt, over-socialising, using violence to address problems, or constantly getting out of it. The spirit finds this excessive behaviour a satisfying fit and so repeats it, whether intensely over one life or less intensely over several lives. However, the enjoyed trait has negative side effects. These eventually lead to psychological wobbles, much like a top towards the end of its spin starts wobbling erratically. In the case of the top, when its wobbles unbalance it completely it falls over and becomes still. Its spinning trajectory ends. Clearly, a spirit cannot fall over in the same way. Whatever it chooses, whatever happens to it, its trajectory continues. But after repeatedly indulged in particular unbalancing psychological behaviours, which in turn feed off self-limiting traits, they have been uploaded to the deep essence and are now embedded in the spirit's accumulated human identity. They will remain there as behavioural patterns, leaking out and unbalancing future lives, until they are addressed. Selecting an essence orientation of repression in order to first restrain, then change those tendencies, provides a practical way to eliminate deeply embedded unbalancing traits.

Where passion intensely throws the individual into particular life situations so life lessons may hit home, repression withdraws the individual from that intensity, creating an inner space so life lessons may have an opportunity to occur. The idea behind this is that when individuals experience powerful external social stimulus they react using their favoured traits. However, if the traits that give rise to self-indulgent behaviours are selected as part of the essence self this time round, but the individual lives a retrained and disengaged life, they are not stimulated. So they are present in the sub-personality but not engaged. The individual now has an opportunity to work on those behaviours, replacing the traits that generate them with positive traits. In this way a new psychological balance is achieved. The repression orientation facilitates this inner growth.

If the self-indulgent traits are very deeply ingrained it may take several lifetimes to achieve a new internal balance. So the repression orientation may need to be adopted for a series of lives. The first one to three lives are usually lived very quietly, in specially selected low-stimulus environments, in an effort to starve the traits. In subsequent lives testing situations will be organised to see if the "wobbler" traits have been sufficiently quelled. If not, a quiet life may again be selected, and new low engagement situations put in place, to allow more time for inner rebalancing.

A word of warning is appropriate here. It cannot be assumed that because a person is living an outwardly restrained life that they have an orientation of repression. There are many reasons an individual chooses a quiet life. Orientation is usually selected in tandem with the life goal, in the context of what essence traits need to be addressed, and taking into account what the spirit decides its accumulated human identity requires to grow. So to understand whether or not a quiet life is being lived by an individual who has an orientation of repression requires knowledge of their current life goal, their most relevant past lives, and what they are seeking to rebalance. An example will clarify what we mean.

Imagine a spirit has a love of music. Over a number of lives it has developed its talent by working as a professional musician, performing and teaching. The opportunities have been positive for enhancing musical skills and learning how to work creatively with others. The many different kinds of social situations the musician has entered have also provided a wide variety of life experiences. All this has promoted positive essence level growth. But alongside this a number of negative self-limiting behaviours have also developed, all forms of self-indulgence. There is petulance when the individual doesn't get its own way. This puts a negative patina on social interactions and inhibits growth. The musician also indulgences in drinking and drug-taking. Finally, when totally strung out, the individual becomes violent. This is a package of behaviours that reinforce one another. By the fourth life of such activity, there is an in-built behavioural tendency imprinted at the level of the accumulated human identity that quickly escalates from petulance to violence. Clearly, this package of behaviours needs to be changed.

For this individual the repression orientation is an extremely useful tool to achieve rebalancing. Several lives will likely be required to eliminate the negative traits and replace them with a package of more positive traits. During this rebalancing period the spirit will likely experience a deep level of frustration, because the life plan limits engagement, yet the spirit has a musical talent that is bursting to manifest. Dealing with frustration then becomes an additional part of the life lesson. How quickly the spirit achieves a psychological rebalancing depends on how hard it works. Self-indulgence can be a difficult trait to transform because at first each new sub-personality is likely to over-indulge in the curative process. This is seen in those who wish to restrain others: they direct their deep desire to transform themselves outwardly towards others instead of inwardly towards themselves, even enjoying the feeling that gives them. In the end, such diversionary behaviour has to be overcome and the underlying personal limitations addressed.

Developmentally, repression is rarely adopted during the mouse and grasshopper phases, simply because not enough has been experienced to generate deeply embedded traits that require adjustment. At times during the grasshopper phase a spirit may adopt the repression orientation to address a negative tendency before it goes too deep, or simply to see what it does to their psyche. However, as with passion, it is during the feline phase that repression is most commonly adopted, because that is when entrenched issues build up and need to be addressed.

Those spirits in the elephant phase utilise repression to help them clear up outstanding psychological issues. But given that spirits nearing the end of their cycle have developed the ability to stand back from their own experiences in the midst of living them, it is usually required for just a life at a time, with a brief adoption being sufficient to achieve the desired rebalancing. Sometimes repression is adopted during the very last lives, when spirits wish to become more inward in their orientation. In this case repression becomes a spiritualising factor in their life—given that "spiritualising" means they are working to bring their spiritual self and their everyday awareness into alignment. Minimising the presence of external distractions fosters this growth.

Unlike what occurs with caution and power, individuals do not swing between passion and repression or seek a balance between them. They are each adopted to help individuals address particular psychological issues that are limiting their progress. In a sense these are stop-go orientations, pushing individuals into intense situations or holding them back from them. No one can or needs to do both simultaneously. Conflicted personalities who engage intensely with life for a time then withdraw are dealing with something else.

AGGRESSION

Aggression and perseverance are dynamic orientations. But all external behaviour reflects inner psychological processes. We are calling these processes traits. It in the psychological trait that manifests in behaviour. But repeated behaviour also alters a trait's inner processing. This is why change is possible. Doing, feeling and thinking are fluid processes that leak into and influence each other. The spirit stands above them, or at least apart from them, and is able to influence them for the better, so they are positive rather then negative, and so the promote growth rather than limit it. The way this works can be seen in the relationship between the aggression trait and violent behaviour.

Violence is the most obvious manifestation of aggression. There is physical violence, verbal violence, and emotional violence, in which one person uses emotional ties to force another to cower. Less obvious is there is also intellectual violence, where ideas are used to obliterate all others that are contrary. There is no doubt that aggression underpins many, but not all, manifestations of violence. After all, people strike out in fear, and parents can go berserk protecting their children. Many sporadically use violence to dominate other people and situations. Within some groups, such as soldiers, violence is perpetrated because it is socially approved, indeed it is socially expected. Nonetheless, let's look at violence as a manifestation of aggression.

People who habitually project violently are seen by others as deliberately in their face and intimidating. But all those in the receiving end of violent behaviour see the external manifestation. In fact, what is happening is that the violence results from the aggressive way the individual processes external stimulus. Others do not respond to the same stimulus in the same way. So the violence is an external manifestation of an internal process. To make a subtle distinction, the violence results from an aggressive reaction more than from an aggressive action—although, clearly, it is both.

However, non-violent aggression is often used to promote essence growth. In professional sports, players are expected to perform with controlled aggression in order to gain an edge over those they are playing. In sport having controlled aggression means playing dynamically, with verve and intensity, but without transgressing the rules, and certainly without becoming violent. Similarly, there is a certain energetic bravado, a derring-do, in the way those with the aggression orientation go at the task of living.

To compare, those with a caution orientation pause and weigh up options before acting, while those with a power orientation strive to dominate a situation or a field of activity or knowledge. Those with a passion orientation intensify engagement to learn life lessons, while those with a repression orientation minimise engagement to give themselves space to transform themselves psychologically. The aggression orientation is selected by those who wish to respond to experiences and situations in a dynamic way.

Take the example of a bulldozer driver. A driver who is enjoying flattening everything in sight might be thought to be aggressively orientated. But the driver might just as easily have a passion, caution or power orientation. The passion individual will be caught up in the experience of driving a powerful machine, the caution individual will enjoy the limited number of decisions he or she has to make, and the power individual may present as the site authority on what needs to be levelled. In contrast, the driver with an aggression orientation will likely be the most dynamic driver, the most daring, the one willing to go to the greatest extreme. Or not. As we keep repeating, underlying traits need to be investigated to be understood. They are never superficially obvious.

The aggression orientation is frequently adopted by spirits during their mouse phase, especially when they have selected a male body and they feel a need to be strong, to have the dynamism, to stand up to threats and to protect themselves and their family. During this phase aggression is adopted by the spirit to defend itself in what it perceives to be a demanding, often threatening, world. Aggression may extend to violent behaviour, or at least to behaviour that projects a willingness to be violent, to keep others at bay.

During the grasshopper phase aggression manifests in two principle forms of behaviour. One is extreme boisterousness, as in the cliche of the cowboys in western movies who drink hard then fight to let off steam. However, others during this phase start learning to internalise aggression and use it to push themselves, to challenge personal limits, and to go further than they would have otherwise. During this phase other traits are usually selected to balance the aggression and to keep the sub-personality from tipping over.

Those in the feline phase of their cycle find the judicious use of aggression is very helpful, especially when they have grown out of its boisterous expression and have learned to internalise it. The feline phase involves judiciously chosen jumps from one life and sub-personality to the next. Focused aggression adds bravado to those jumps, leading to the resulting experiences being much more expansive and having greater depth than otherwise. On the other hand, if the individual is unable to focus the aggression orientation then the result is usually messy, with unplanned karmic debts being generated. Spirits in this phase who wish to select the aggression orientation are usually prepared beforehand, either with between-life training or, more commonly, by building up to it through trying out related traits before finally adopting aggression. But, of course, there are always some who select aggression, close their eyes, jump into their next body and personality, and see what results.

Those in the elephant phase rarely select aggression, unless they have a specific issue or situation they wish to address and they need the deering-do that aggression offers. However, their vast store of experience inevitably softens the externally grating effects of aggression, with the result that in most cases the aggression is barely discernible.

PERSEVERANCE

The perseverance orientation complements aggression. It involves absorbing life's storms and staying on course without being distracted. It is steady and unspectacular compared to the deering-do generated by the aggression orientation, but just like aggression it helps individuals get the job done.

To compare perseverance and aggression, the fable of the hare and the tortoise is appropriate. The hare moves abruptly and goes a long way in a single bound, whereas the tortoise plods along. Each has its strengths and weaknesses. The hare can get too daring and extend itself too far. Then it gets into so much trouble it is unable to do what it is aiming to. The tortoise, in working slowly but surely to complete its tasks, can become too finnicky over details. This may have repercussions later in life if later tasks depend on earlier stages being completed in a timely fashion. In each case the life plan is not completed. For the hare it is as a result of bravado getting it into a situation it could extract itself from, and for the hare it is because of perfectionism or just being too slow.

Individuals adopt the orientation of perseverance as a way of adding backbone to their accumulated human identity, just as they adopt aggression to add energy and to shake off conservative tendencies. Learning focus is one of the core skills, because without it inner depth cannot be developed. The persistence that comes with perseverance helps to learn focus.

Of course, all this presupposes that individuals hear and act on the urges emanating from their essence self. Given the variety of urges that enter the everyday awareness from the biological and socialised selves, hearing then acting on what the essence self says can itself be difficult to do. What happens in each life is that the sub-personality will feel a persistent urge prompting it from deep within, usually without knowing where the urge comes from. Individuals feel compelled to orient themselves in the way the inner urges them, whether cautiously, passionately, powerfully, aggressively, and so on. The earlier in life individuals open themselves up to that orientation the more it will come through and influence their life in the way that the spirit planned.

However, in many lives external circumstances inhibit the expression of essence urges. Inhibition resulting from a religious upbringing is common, as is a materialist upbringing that denies the validity of subtle urges. In these cases, there will likely come a time in an individual's life when their spiritual self gives them a wake up call and they feel an urgent drive to express deep urges. At this point in the life journey a struggle with ensue, a struggle we have already discussed in terms of a war between two streams, the stream of socialised and physical existence, and the stream of essence existence. In order for the selected orientation to steer one's life, a jump has to be made in which everyday awareness shifts its grounding to the essence stream.

How easily the jump is done, and especially what has to be fought against to achieve it, is always part of the life plan. It may be that the jump is only completed late in life, too late to substantially change that life. This is not a wasted effort. Far from it. What happens in this case is that a new pattern for inner change is initiated. When the sub-personality and its body die, this new pattern is uploaded to the store of deep essence and so becomes part of that individual's accumulated human identity. With the pattern in place, even if it is only weakly, it is now available to be drawn on in the next life. Each time the pattern is repeated in a life it is uploaded again, and so becomes more strongly embedded at the deep essence level. Each time the spirit's sub-personalities find it progressively easier to adopt that pattern.

This is why it usually takes a number of lives to bed in newly adjusted traits. The orientation traits initiate new patterns of behaviour, but the spirit has to learn how to balance the trait and its personality behaviours with life's distractions. No one gets any change right first time.

Everyone tries all orientations at some time during their incarnation cycle. However, perseverance applies best when individuals are seeking to apply and develop specific skills and abilities. Perseverance helps individuals complete goals, especially exacting goals that require several lives for all their intricacies to be explored. This means the perseverance orientation becomes more attractive as spirits accumulate more experience. Hence it is more often selected in the second half of the incarnation cycle than the first.

During the mouse phase the point is to experience, so perseverance is not often adopted. It may be chosen for a life or two to help steady sub-personalities that tend towards instability, especially if fear has dominated previous lives and generated a behavioural pattern of skitteriness. The perseverance orientation helps compensate for this.

During the grasshopper phase aggression is more often adopted than perseverance, because this phase is about being adventurous. Nonetheless, many individuals, who are not innately adventurous due to the make-up of their core disposition, prefer perseverance because they like the limitation in scope and the orderliness and consistency of purpose that it urges them into. The grasshopper phase involves experimenting with various skills, so individuals may also select perseverance to help them embed skills they are enjoying.

Perseverance provides a natural balance during the feline stage. This is when individuals are adding depth and breadth to their skills base, extending their knowledge base, working across sequences of lives to transform abilities into talents, attempting to establish truly loving relationships, and throughout it all are opening up their lives beyond the concerns of their sub-personality by integrating input from their spiritual self. This is all too much to attempt in each and every life. Accordingly, during the feline phase life plans are drawn up to deal with small packages of related issues across a sequence of lives. The feline leap comes in when the individual enters a new series of situations. Aggression can initially be useful to help the individual become at ease facing challenging new life lessons, because having deering-do gives them confidence. Subsequently perseverance becomes useful, helping the individual bed down the lessons and integrate them at the deep essence level.

This is another example of how sliding between paired traits is useful. A significant aim of incarnation is learning to respond appropriately in any situation. Knowing when to jump daringly and when to work quietly but persistently is one small aspect of this much larger aim. Many people leap when they should plod and plod when they should leap. The only way to become dextrous is to repeatedly attempt each. What is learned then becomes embedded as a behavioural pattern in the individual's accumulated human identity, which may then be drawn on in subsequent lives. Life lessons lead to the accumulated human identity maturing and progressively becoming more refined.

During the elephant phase unfinished business from previous lives is completed. This includes integrating talents through all layers of the self, capping off fields of knowledge, bringing relationships to sweet conclusions, and resolving karma. It will be clear that the perseverance orientation would be very helpful throughout this process, and so it is often chosen.

OBSERVATION

Caution and observation are the most frequently chosen orientations. Well over half the human population currently possesses one or the other. This is understandable, because human life is difficult enough without seeking the more complex scenarios that the other orientations lead to.

Caution results in individuals processing carefully before acting, while observation steers people into the neutral behaviour of standing back and watching what is happening. However, selecting the observation orientation doesn't mean individuals don't engage with life. There are many other traits functioning within the layered self, some of which may drive individuals into extreme life situations. The point of tentative caution and neutral observation is that they help individuals "cool down" their responses as they steer a course through life's often tempestuous waters. Psychologically, they reduce the unbalancing tendencies generated by more reactive and extreme traits.

The caution and observation orientations are also prevalent because the majority of the human population is currently in either the grasshopper or early feline phases of their incarnation cycles. This means they are either engaged in tasting a variety of experiences, or are just beginning to organise their previous experiences by selecting judiciously from them and developing them. Caution and observation steady their life courses. As the human population matures the predominant orientations will change to reflect what best suits the majority of individuals in the later phases of their incarnation cycles.

Observation is the most uncomplicated orientation. When major issues arise, which temporarily shock individuals out of their socialised self and into their essence self, they will not be as reactive as those who possess any of the other orientations besides caution. Of course, in practice few people are completely non-reactive. As we just observed, other psychological traits exist in the layered self that also influence behaviour. In addition, the biological and socialised selves are inherently reactive to extreme life situations. So what we mean by the observation orientation being less reactive is simply that individuals take in what is happening around them and to them, but at the essence level they don't jump into immediate action themselves. They wait, and watch. Ideally, they don't just watch others, they also watch themselves. The result is a simpler essence level psychological momentum.

In our model of the essence self as a boat, we likened the life goal to the ballast that brings the boat back onto an even keel when troubled waters are encountered. Orientation we likened to the rudder that steers the boat around obstacles and brings it back onto course. For most people ballast and rudder, life goal and orientation, work together in a complex interplay. When an individual has selected the observation orientation to steer its boat, the individual has an innate essence level tendency not to respond when life becomes intense. Then the usual interplay between orientation and life goal is reduced, and the life goal predominates. This is why we stated that observation is the simplest orientation. It simplifies essence level decision-making, allowing other traits to come to the fore. This is what makes observation a self-neutralising trait.

Observation's simplifying tendency makes it useful in any phase of the incarnation cycle. For those in the mouse phase, observation helps when individuals want to stay out of trouble. Less likely to be drawn into life's hurley-burly, they are freer to watch how others use skills and the ways social norms play out in the human world. It is often said that children learn by imitating those around them. For those in the mouse phase, the observation orientation promotes learning by imitating.

For those in the grasshopper phase there are times when the intensity of life experiences becomes too much. This applies to a sequence of lives as much as to a sequence of days or weeks. During such periods individuals want to step down the intensity of their life engagement. This enables them to catch their breath and gives them space to integrate experiences into their current sub-personality. Observation is an ideal orientation to do this. Naturally, other supportive and complementary traits also need to be selected to allow inner breathing space to occur.

This need to catch up with one's prior experiences also applies during the feline phase. However, there is a potential complication. This is that as an individual's experiential store grows so do the numbers of traits that have been "tried on" during earlier lives. A number of these traits will have generated defensive behavioural patterns that are now stored in the deep essence. Examples of such behaviours include being emotionally bristly to keep others at a distance, or sustaining suspicion so one does not get trapped in situations where one is exploited, or worse. As the individual matures these kinds of defensive traits become limiting because they stop the individual engaging in new growth-promoting experiences. The difficulty is that over a series of lives these defensive behaviours have become "go to" traits. That is, they have become an individual's preferred psychological means of keeping life's trivial annoyances at arm's length. As a result they have been repeated many times and are now embedded in the individual's accumulated human identity. Before these traits can be changed they first have to be perceived in operation. The observation orientation is very useful for doing so. If a number of interlinked behaviours are being changed, several lives will be required to eliminate them all. In this case observation may be adopted repeatedly until psychological transformation is under way. Other orientations will then be adopted to bed in the replacement behaviours.

By the mid-elephant phase individuals have usually repeated the observation orientation sufficiently that the behavioural pattern of self-observation is embedded in their deep essence. Accordingly, the observation orientation is not as necessary as during the grasshopper and feline phases. Mature individuals who do choose observation tend to be tolerant, so their observations come with humour and even sly knowingness. Individuals in this phase have also learned how to involve themselves in life without losing themselves. A part of them is always watching, the silent observer of their own and others' successes, struggles and follies.

CHAPTER 9

Adopting an Attitude
Towards Life

E VERYONE NEEDS A WAY TO CUT THROUGH THE CONSTANT WASH
of life that froths around them. Attitude provides a psychological trait
to do precisely that. On the one hand, attitude is a defence mechanism, a
way to avoid having to give equal attention to every little thing life throws
up. On the other, attitude gives each personality a particular angle on life,
what could almost be called a psychological agenda, that it uses to get where
it is going without becoming bogged down with what is peripheral for it. So
while attitude is defensive in the sense that it steers the boat of the essence
self away from waters that don't appeal to it, it does so in order to help the
individual fulfil its life plan. This is a complex idea to communicate, so we'll
expand.

Think of the bow of a boat cutting through the water. Water offers resistance to the boat's forward momentum. Bows may be narrow or broad,
suited to racing or cruising, be straight or curved, go deep under the water or
be mostly above water. However shaped, the bow is designed to reduce water
resistance. If the boat didn't have a bow, if it was shaped like an oblong box,
the resistance would be too great to move with any great speed. In addition,
navigation would be limited, navigation being the ability to head in a chosen
direction and respond to hazards in the water by steering around them. The
bow facilitates the boat's maneuverability and enables it to sail rather than
merely bump and drift.

This is also the case with an individual human being. Attitude provides
a bow that helps it cut through the resistance that daily life provides. How-

ever, where a boat is physical, human identity is psychological. And the human psychology doesn't just steer through and around experiences, it always absorbs something from what it experiences.

To add another metaphor, attitude may be thought of as a filter. Imagine seven people in the same situation, who have the same sensory, emotional and intellectual sea available to them. But each has a different attitude, each cuts through the water with a differently shaped bow. Psychologically, each steers towards some of the available experiences and away from others. And each filters what it experiences, absorbing information along the way. So attitude is instrumental to what kinds of experiences individuals steer into and away from, and to what each absorbs from its experiences.

This is attitude as it is experienced from inside the human personality. From the outside, attitude is perceived as the psychological angle other people use to come at life. Many misunderstandings and collisions occur between people because of differences in their psychological angles. Accordingly, appreciating attitude has a two-fold purpose. It helps you understand

THE SEVEN ATTITUDES

	(+)	(−)
SELF-ACTUALISING		
REALIST	Perception	Supposition
CYNIC	Contradiction	Denigration
SELF-TRANSFORMING		
SRIRITUALIST	Verification	Faith
STOIC	Tranquility	Resignation
SELF-FULFILLING		
IDEALIST	Coalesence	Abstraction
SCEPTIC	Investigation	Suspicion
SELF-NEUTRALISING		
PRAGMATIST	Practicality	Dogma

FIGURE 7.1

why others take the angle on life that they do, and it helps you understand why you yourself have a particular angle on life. Of course, other factors impact on anyone's angle. Life goal and orientation join with attitude to form an essence level unit that drives you from birth to death. They work together to help you fulfil your plans along the way. But before you can appreciate how the three work together, you first have to decipher each part of the puzzle.

Again we draw on the Michael Teachings to identify the seven attitudes. They fall into three pairs: the self-actualising realist and cynic, the self-transformational spiritualist and stoic, the self-fulfilling idealist and sceptic, and the self-neutralising pragmatist.

You likely have little difficulty recognising the idealist, stoic, cynic, or pragmatist among people you know. This is because, as we have noted, attitude flows from the essence self into the socialised self, and the socialised self's characteristics are the most easily recognised. Identifying and appreciating the purpose of particular attitudes is extremely useful because it offers a way into the hidden parts of the essence self, thereby illuminating yourself and others. We'll start by discussing the self-actualising pair of realist and cynic.

REALIST

Simply, the realist is the person who perceives the lay of the land and does what it takes to get the job done. But we mean this in a particular sense. The pragmatist also gets things done. The difference between them is the pragmatist grabs whatever is at hand and uses it to do what is required. In contrast, the realist has a broader perception of what is at hand, being able to see what is ahead that might help or impede getting the job done. So the realist is able to strategise more than the pragmatist. Of course, all this depends on how much experience individuals have, how many prior lives they have dealt with the same situations they are now facing, and how deeply they are able to look into what is around them. So other traits impact weakly or more strongly on their realism.

Realists don't like having the wool pulled over their eyes. The realist attitude clears the air, enabling individuals to perceive without either rose or grey-tinted glasses. Realists can be brutally honest at times, not to get at others but because they like to be up-front about what they perceive. If they possess other traits that push them to communicate, then they will share their perceptions with brutal honesty. This can create problems if those around them don't want honesty, and also if in their interactions they draw on different sensibilities. This may be the situation with idealists and spiritualists who don't have the same desire to view what is in front of them because their gaze is fixed on what is ahead.

Where realists get into psychological trouble is when they think they are being honest but they are really drawing on suppositions derived from what is inside their head. Instead of perceiving reality, they project preconceptions onto reality. This is particularly the case when individuals have been conditioned into a particular outlook, whether religious, political, body-based, and so on. Their realistic attitude then becomes a projected prejudice or discriminatory attitude that acts as an obstacle trait. It will often be a powerful obstacle, because when individuals have other strong traits driving them their suppositions become bullheaded and pugnacious. If that trait is subsequently uploaded to deep essence it becomes an obstacle that takes considerable effort to purify and transform.

The realist attitude is adopted at any time during the incarnation cycle. An immature realist is something of a blunt instrument. Such an individual clearly perceives what is happening, but not at much depth, so its statements reflect a crude level of understanding. A mature realist is like a dancing scimitar, responding thrust to thrust to what life throws at them, but doing so with artistry and finesse. The immature realist's comments are truthful, but their truth is limited and delivered bluntly so can cut and hurt, whereas the mature realist offers truthful and deep observations that build others up rather than cut them down.

For those in the mouse stage, the realist attitude is a two-edged knife. It enables the individual to realistically face up to whatever is going on around it. However, because the mouse phase spirit doesn't have a grounding stock of experiences, seeing too clearly can be highly unsettling, especially if the social environment is stark and tough. For this spirit being realistic is likely to fan fears and so suppress endeavour instead of stimulating it. Naturally, this self-suppressing response also depends on the spirit's core disposition. A spirit with a warrior disposition and an action modality might deliberately adopt the realistic attitude to bolster its innate energy and give it further strength to act. If a different spirit, say with a sage core disposition and a meditative modality, adopts the realist attitude during this phase, it is likely to be within a highly structured and genteel social environment, the purpose being to see through the pretensions to a deeper level—because spirits during all four phases have periods when they wish to look, feel and think at a deeper level than the superficial.

During the grasshopper phase the realist attitude is adopted to provide a clear view of the environment into which an individual is leaping. As in the mouse phase, adopting the realist attitude is like taking off tinted glasses and clearly seeing what one is faced with. This is useful when working on an obstacle, whether external or internal, because the first step to solving a problem is facing up to it.

In the feline phase the realistic attitude comes into its own because it sharpens the sub-personality's perceptions and helps it cut to the chase when considering the circumstances of its life and what has to be done. During the grasshopper phase there are more randomly selected one-off lives in which the spirit tries a little of this and a little of that. As the grasshopper spirit matures it starts selecting short series of lives so it can bed-in abilities and desired traits. During the feline phase lives are mostly organised into larger sequences in order to bed-in life lessons and to get serious developmental work done. The realist attitude is extremely useful for achieving these goals. The realist attitude is adopted at the start of a sequence of lives, to put what is being worked on into sharp relief, or it is chosen in the middle of a sequence of lives in order to bring the purpose of this sequence back into focus, or it is selected at the end of the sequence to really hit home the life lesson or complete a specific task.

During the elephant phase the realist attitude has the same developmental purpose, being used to address karmic issues and resolve them, or to highlight outstanding inner traits and their deficiencies. The main difference between the feline and elephant phases is that the feline gaze is often directed outwardly, into the circumstances of life, because the spirit is still grappling with how to develop a balance between satisfying inward desires and drives and adjusting the outward impact of what the individual chooses to do. Ironically, the realist attitude is often adopted by those in the elephant phase who are having difficulty coping with the the way their inner spiritual abilities and understanding are developing. For example, towards the end of their full cycle spirits gain insights into past lives, come to appreciate how they have shaped themselves as a result of past life choices, and start developing various intuitive abilities, especially becoming able to see more deeply into their own and others' past lives than they were able to before. This deep information can be unsettling. Adopting a realist attitude, which helps the individual view intuitive spiritual level information matter-of-factly, can help counter the unsettling nature of these insights. This is why we say it is ironic: a realistic attitude aids the assimilation of intuitions that many people claim are unreal.

CYNIC

The cynic attitude is at the other extreme from the realist. Both attitudes share a tendency to be brutally honest, but where the realist is often admired, the cynic is the victim of a bad press. The cynic is widely seen as negative, even destructive. This is to misunderstand what the cynic attitude involves.

As with the realist attitude, the cynic looks hard at the world but, as we have said, how far or how deeply depends on prior experience and on the individual's other essence traits. The investigative journalist is a cynic in the best sense, not happy to accept what appears to be the case, and certainly not willing to accept superficial explanations. The hard-bitten cynical journalist who has seen and heard it all was something of a cliche in the second half of the twentieth century, being the hero, or at least the leading character, in fiction and films, and something of a role-model for those who thought it was a social good to "speak truth to power."

It could be said that post-modern analysis involves a cynical approach, confronting people with the assumptions that underpin their actions and with the consequences of what they are doing. During that time, and we are thinking of the period from post-World War 2 to 9-11, the cynic had social space to say what they thought. These days, and we are writing in the second decade of the twenty-first century, that space is much more constricted. The limitations of cynical post-modern critiques are now being revealed, because once old attitudes and actions have been pulled down and taken apart, the next task is to build new attitudes and initiate new actions. This is a task for which deconstructive post-modernism is not naturally equipped. In addition, the current media environment is less supportive of those who would "speak truth to power." Investigative journalism does not have the prominence it had last century, and the hard-bitten cynical journalist is no longer as common. Instead, the cynical social commentator is more commonly seen in the arena of stand-up comedy. While there is considerable freedom for individuals to use the comic environment to make truthful observations, the impact is not the same as it would be if the observations were being communicated via media headlines. Investigative journalism has itself largely been banished from mainstream media, appearing in quality but lower circulation newspapers and online platforms. In this way the positive contributions made by deep-seeing cynics is sidelined. Nonetheless, their knowledgable views are available for those who need a dose of reality from time to time.

The realist and cynic attitudes are equally dynamic. Both address the world in its rough and tumble reality. But the realist is more externally focused while the cynic is more inwardly focused. Where realists see things as they are then use their observations to get things done, cynics see things as they are then use their observations to call attention to what is being done badly, immorally, or under false premises. To put it perhaps overly simplistically, the realist says, "You can do it and this is how," whereas the cynic says, "No, you're not doing it and this is why." Naturally, others don't enjoy being brought face to face with social, economic, systemic or personal shortcomings, so there is always push back to those articulating a cynical attitude—unless they are in a forum like stand-up comedy and their observations can be "fenced off" from daily life.

The cynical attitude is overwhelmingly a mature response to human existence. Those in their mouse phase have no great use for playing the cynic, chiefly because they don't have the experiential stocks to perceive what is happening around them with any depth. Similarly, those in their grasshopper phase are more concerned with getting things right in an everyday sense, and in honing their skills. They don't need the ability to look deeply and cynically into the world to achieve their goals.

However, during the feline phase spirits' sub-personalities have explored many human possibilities, have built up an extensive experiential store, and are beginning to develop a nuanced view of human existence. The cynical attitude is very useful for adding depth to perceptions, and also in itself generates a compelling life experience. After all, investigative journalists today who address corporate malfeasance or state-level lying, and then have to deal with the blowback that results from their reports, have intense, multi-level life experiences that challenge them emotionally and intellectually and, if they are imprisoned for what they produce, physically and psychologically.

During the elephant phase the realist attitude is more likely to be adopted than the cynic. This because the cynical attitude is more useful for deconstructing outlooks than building them up, and the final phase is about putting it all together psychospiritually. A notable exception is when spirits enter the final elephant phase without having addressed fundamental self-limiting aspects of their accumulated human identity and, speaking figuratively, they need a dose of smelling salts to wake them up to what is going on within. Adopting the cynic attitude for a life or two helps them see more deeply into everyday life and to be confronted by their shortcomings. In this case, the cynic attitude would be adopted for its self-remedial qualities.

As with orientations, the pairs of attitudes function within sliding scales. The realist requires cynical insight into the world to better perceive what it is faced with, while the cynical can't just wallow in their insights but need to put what they see into action. Accordingly, these attitudes are often used in tandem, across a short series of lives, to hone the ability to analyse and to develop an ability to cope with and keep working through tricky situations. Those who are able to deeply and critically observe, and use their observations to adjust how they steer through complex life situations, are mature spirits.

STOIC

Everyone has met an individual who carries on in a sanguine mood even when life is falling apart around them. This is the stoic. The stoic leads with his or her chin, takes life's blows, and carries on regardless. This is their way of cutting through life's churned waters. Historically, the Greeks took this trait to such an extreme that they adopted it as a life philosophy, and so the terms "stoicism" and "being stoic" have entered the English language. Clearly, and given there are six other attitudes, being stoic is not for everyone, although not flinching in the face of problems would be a psychological plus for everyone. This is why all individuals adopt the stoic attitude many times during their incarnation cycle.

The negative manifestation of stoicism is resignation. Resignation is the psychological equivalent of turning off your boat's engine, coming to a halt, and allowing life's swells to buffet you however they will. This is not the idea of being a stoic. A spirit uses its stoic sub-personality's ability to stay sanguine and not to flinch in order to keep moving forwards to achieve its goals. There is no giving up for the fully functioning stoic.

At least, this is the ideal. In practice, it takes effort to remain stoic in the face of difficulties. When you first adopt an attitude or an orientation it doesn't mean your new sub-personality is automatically able to apply it successfully and naturally in its life. Each time you need to learn how to do so. This makes the stoic attitude a self-transformational trait. Spirits adopt it when learning to be stoical in the face of life difficulties will help them develop other aspects of their accumulated human identity. It usually takes multiple attempts to learn to be stoical.

The stoic attitude also needs to be adopted periodically, because as you accumulate more experiences you also develop both positive and self-limiting traits in response to those experiences. These periodically need to be adjusted into a new psychological balance. The stoic attitude, which establishes a stable internal platform for psychological change, is particularly useful to rebalancing. Accordingly, it is a go-to attitude for all spirits during all phases of their incarnation cycle.

The stoic attitude is adopted during the mouse phase of incarnation as it helps the spirit maintain consistent forward momentum. During their first lives spirits have little inner strength to draw on. Consequently, they tend to react to each and every incident that occurs. Clearly, this is not useful if they wish to complete life tasks. A stoic attitude gives them psychological strength to cope with variable life situations.

During the more adventurous grasshopper phase stoicism is a go-to attitude for some and is avoided by others. This split occurs because many not only wish to start leaping into new experiences, they wish to experience them intensely. Stoicism naturally dampens down intensity, so they avoid it. Conversely, other spirits find the grasshopper phase somewhat chaotic. They seek out the company of others, sticking to groups and stable social and work environments that provide consistency and predictability, so they can test and extend themselves in a more orderly fashion, little by little, in more placid, predictable life situations. When they can't organise this type of environment, adopting stoicism provides them with a sort of psychological envelope that protects them in the same way that being in a group usually does.

The stoic attitude is also very useful during the feline phase, when spirits are working to fulfil specific tasks and being able to shrug off incidental vicissitudes and stay focused is very useful. The stoic attitude is adopted during the feline phase to finish off particular projects, whether that involves developing an ability, achieving a physical, emotional or intellectual goal, or addressing psychological traits. Given spirits during this phase select sequences of lives to get things done, stoicism is often used judiciously at particular points during a sequence, to steady the boat, so to speak, and to keep momentum going.

During the elephant phase the stoic attitude is a favourite because it aids inner transformation. It is also consistent with the mature spirit's outlook, which is that much of life's pettiness is not worth expending time and energy on. So those in the elephant phase have a natural desire to breeze past troubled waters. The stoic attitude reinforces this breezy approach to life.

The feline phase proportionally takes up more lives than any of the other phases. This is because growing from immature adult to mature adult, which is equivalent to aging from twenty-one to sixty-five or more in the physical human cycle, involves the greatest amount of life experiences and also generates the most issues that consequently need to be worked through and resolved. The feline phase is when skills are honed into abilities and when abilities manifest as exceptional talents. It is also when responsibilities are at their greatest, when life is at its most demanding, and is often when individual spirits achieve the most. Accordingly, during this phase each spirit takes on all seven attitudes, even if some are not a natural or easy fit, and we're referring to the attitudes of cynic and spiritualist in particular here, which many find difficult to sustain. The seven attitudes naturally divide into those that keep sub-personalities grounded in the world and those that lift them out of the world. The spiritualist attitude is one of the latter traits.

SPIRITUALIST

The stoic attitude is straightforward. The attitude with which it is paired is not. This is because there is much misunderstanding regarding what being spiritual involves. It is certainly not the same as being religious. Religion involves socialised worship of the divine. Spirituality involves a direct encounter with the divine, which occurs when an individual creates an inner liaison with the spiritual self. As a result of doing so the individual internally redefines the spiritual—because it may be said that in general religious statements about the divine and what it actually is when directly experienced are not the same. The rigidity associated with religion does not apply to spirituality. Of course, many worshippers do not share their religion's rigidity. They are engaged in religious activities because it helps them become more spiritual. All this not only creates confusion regarding what the spiritualist attitude involves, it may also make life more difficult for those who adopt it.

The paired attitudes of stoic and spiritualist are self-transformational. They are adopted to help the individual transform themselves. The stoic attitude helps because it enables individuals to shrug off non-essential inputs and keep working on the task at hand. The spiritualist attitude does the same thing by enabling individuals to rise above non-essentials. Simply, where stoics have their eye on a distant prize, spiritualists have their eye on a higher prize.

The spiritualist attitude is adopted by those who wish to actively include their spiritual self in their life plan. It might be thought that this would lead to involvement in a religion. In fact, this is not necessarily the case. Individuals can use any occupation to develop their connection with their spiritual self. Visual artists, writers, architects, gardeners, physicists, social workers, teachers, in fact anyone in any walk of life, can use their occupation as a means to develop the connection between their everyday awareness and their spiritual self. In practice, selecting a spiritualist attitude, then incarnating within a religious social environment, is frequently problematic because the disparity between worshippers' felt experience and religious doctrine often generates friction. Being openly questioning, which those with a spiritualist attitude often feel compelled to do, can have serious personal, family and community consequences. Of course, those who adopt a spiritualist attitude and choose to be incarnated into a religious environment deliberately do so to experience such conflicts.

Given the spiritualist attitude may be adopted in a wide range of social contexts, it is necessary to identify its key characteristics. Essentially, the spiritualist attitude involves seeking higher meanings, higher experiences, and higher understanding of the world. These meanings, experiences and understanding do not have to be what is generally considered spiritual or religious. It may involve peering into the interior workings of the natural world, as was done by Isaac Newton and Albert Einstein. It may involve psychological investigation, as was practised by Carl Jung. It may involve medicine, or horticulture, or environmental issues. The key is that the investigation has the purpose of discovering higher orders of otherwise invisible activity and pattern.

The spiritualist attitude is frequently paired with the life goal of growth, because it involves the individual in tasks selected to facilitate personal growth. Where sub-personalities with an attitude of spiritualist lose their way is when their spiritual impulse is diverted into the promulgation or defence of faith, whether that faith involves religious or other forms of doctrines. Then the goal of personal growth becomes blunted, the personality loses its momentum and its goals for this life are not realised. Such diversion is common, especially when a sub-personality is born into a religious community and powerful social conditioning forges a rigid socialised self, which then controls the everyday awareness, keeping at bay the cues given by the spiritual self. This is why many individual spirits choose to utilise their spiritual attitude outside a specifically religious environment. This is especially so during the more mature phases of the incarnation cycle.

Few individuals choose the spiritualist attitude during their field mouse phase because they are working on developing the basic skills needed to live in the human domain. They are also still grappling with the hormonal surges that flow through the human biology, surges they have difficulty controlling. So most see no point in adopting a spiritualist attitude. Those who take up religious vows during this phase do so not to establish an experiential connection between their everyday awareness and their spiritual self but because they want the shelter and order a religious environment provides. It is external safety, not the inner divine, that spirits seek during their mouse phase.

During the grasshopper phase, the spiritualist attitude helps intensify experiences. Because these spirits do not yet have a deep experiential store, the insights they achieve are rarely profound, but they do lay the foundations for deep explorations in later lives. However, only a minority of spirits want to peer more deeply into the nature of human experience during the grasshopper phase, and those who do tend to be expressing their core disposition. For example, the scholars' innate desire to understand may lead them into deep explorations. Those with an inward modality may also be driven to explore their spiritual self earlier than is the norm. Of course, there is no ultimate advantage to those who do so. It is just the way their core disposition tends.

During the feline phase, spirits experience a great deal on multiple levels. Learning to access their spiritual self is just one of many skills that need to be acquired. At some stage all spirits have to address their deeper self. The spiritualist attitude helps them do so. However, for some this may come quite late in the feline phase, while for others it is earlier. Having an essence level drive to rise above daily issues can psychologically destabilise a subpersonality, so many spirits choose to work on integrating their spiritual self into their everyday awareness quite late in their overall cycle. The reason is simply that life is difficult enough without adding a spiritual dimension. There is some advantage to this strategy, given that later in their overall cycle they have an extensive experiential store to draw on, have worked through much of their karma, and are also likely to have a reasonably balanced accumulated human identity. This makes introducing their spiritual self into their everyday awareness much easier to achieve. Those who are more adventurous and adopt a spiritualist outlook in their early feline or even late grasshopper phases usually get into more trouble. On the other hand, they have experiences and life lessons that others do not.

The elephant phase provides a crucial period of inner growth. For those at any stage of their incarnational cycle who have not explored their spiritual level to any great depth, adopting the spiritualist attitude can be ungrounding. They may internally feel like they have been lifted out of their direct connection with the world around them. If the world they are living in is ruptured by powerful currents, such as war or cultural revolutions, individuals who adopt the spiritualist attitude but lack a relevant experiential grounding can fall psychologically, perhaps very hard. This is a disincentive that holds individuals back from exploring their spiritual dimension and so disinclines them to adopt the spiritualist attitude. However, by the time spirits enter their elephant phase they have an extensive store of experiences. This store grounds them internally, so when they adopt the spiritualist attitude they naturally have a greater ability to keep their spiritual self and their everyday personality in balance.

An exception is when spirits really haven't prepared themselves at all for meeting their own spiritual aspect in the human world. In such a case a period of adjustment is required, which can be unnerving for the spirit's sub-personalities. The advantage is that the adjustment period is much shorter during the elephant phase than during earlier phases. However it is achieved, the end result is an integration of the spiritual self and the everyday awareness, with all the deeper knowledge that releases.

IDEALIST

The paired attitudes of idealist and sceptic are self-fulfilling, in the sense that each gives expression to higher impulses, but they do so in different ways. To distinguish between them in very general terms, the idealist is life-affirming and seeks to strengthen people's place in the world, whereas sceptics are critical, often undercutting others hopes and dreams, particularly by highlighting their illusions. Of course this is a crude demarcation, because idealists also present a challenge to norms and the status quo, of which they are often sceptical, while sceptics have an idealistic motivation, given that no one critiques questionable situations or others' actions unless they ultimately think there could be a better way of doing things. We'll return to this distinction shortly.

People with an idealist attitude are often instantly identifiable, as they put "their heads above the parapet" by performing the valuable social function of bell-ringers and reminding everyone that greater possibilities exist. Many non-government organisations, such as Greenpeace and Doctors Without Borders, are manifestations of the idealist attitude as they seek to socially actualise higher perspectives and impulses. Others are idealists on a smaller scale, but are often equally visible within their personal and occupational circles.

This is the sense in which idealists are self-fulfilling: they work to give visible social expression to the higher level impulses that drive them. Ultimately, such impulses emanate from the spiritual self as it lovingly seeks to express what it has learned and understands. This means the idealist attitude is also aspirational, given that idealists identify goals for themselves and everyone else to aspire to—goals that may be environmental, economic, practical, cultural or psychological—then work to put them into action.

Because of the prevalence of worldwide media and the ease of international communications, today idealist individuals and organisations can spread their message and become involved globally as well as locally. The idealist attitude may take an intellectual form, manifesting philosophically in the fields of ethics, economics or environmental care, seeking to identify and make others aware of key drivers each. Or the idealist may be driven by health concerns, and so function socially in the area of social policy or provide psychological support. In these cases the idealist attitude is more emotional in expression. Idealists may alternatively provide direct medical support to the needy or for those who are disadvantaged by changing environmental conditions, perhaps by building houses or providing seeds and access to water for crops. In this case idealism has a very physical application. These examples indicate how the expression of the idealist attitude, like all attitudes, is impacted by core disposition, life goal, essence preferences, and other traits. However, what unites all cases is that the idealist always strives to give abstract ideals visible expression in the world.

The negative aspect of idealism occurs when a person's ideals remain abstract, usually as a result of not being fully expressed in worldly activity. Fear is a fundamental inhibitor of an individual's expression of any attitude, which results when false personality and the limiting traits surrounding chief feature dominate an individual's everyday awareness. Such a person will first become inwardly frustrated, then will manifest negative behaviour, the form of which depends on what other psychological traits are present, and the nature of their core disposition and its modality. For example, if such a person possesses a warrior disposition and an action modality, they will perhaps lash out and strive to dominate others with their idealised perspective. Another with a servant disposition and a life goal of self-deprecation whose everyday awareness is dominated by their false personality may have their idealism go inwardly sour, resulting in an embittered sense of futility, that nothing can really be done to right the world. Nothing is more tortured—and torturing to others—than an idealist whose drive is thwarted by their awareness of their own inadequacies. The Inquisition is an example of the idealist impulse that became so abstracted from living conditions that it lost its connection to fellow feeling and sought to force its intolerant moral pattern on the human world.

Like the spiritualist and cynic attitudes, the idealist attitude requires a reasonable depth of experience before it becomes useful. Accordingly, it is rarely adopted by those in the field mouse phase of their incarnational cycle. An exception is when individuals feel they need to connect with their deeper impulses. The difference between the spiritualist and idealist attitudes is that the spiritualist seeks a personal self-transformational experience whereas the idealist strives to make a higher ideal manifest in the world. One is more generally personally orientated, the other more socially oriented—although, of course, the opposite may also be the case. Those in the mouse phase generally lack the experience to appreciate the nuances involved in putting an ideal into action, but opportunities may become available during this phase that they decide to adopt the idealist attitude, especially if they possess a core disposition that is naturally adventurous.

The same applies during the grasshopper phase. The difference between the field mouse and grasshopper phases is that by the latter phase spirits have accrued a range of experience, so for them to adopt an idealist attitude and join a group of like-minded individuals working collectively at a cause offers them a distinctive and exciting life experience that helps them start opening up their deeper impulses rather than a too challenging one. Those with a servant core disposition would likely use the opportunity to serve others, warriors would use it as a cause to do battle for, scholars may find exploring the cause's history and ramifications fascinating, and a sage would have a platform on which to perform. Idealists are always in the minority, with a handful usually being more than enough for others around them to cope with, but they are essential contributors to the advancement of human culture. For this reason, the idealist attitude is often linked to the life goal of growth in both the grasshopper and feline phases.

Those in the grasshopper phase who chose the idealist attitude usually do so within a supportive group context, aligning themselves with others who have adopted the same trait. In contrast, those in the feline phase, and especially those who are in the latter half of this phase, are more confident of their skills and so are often content to select the idealist attitude and use it to function more independently. How independently depends on how far they wish to challenge themselves, given lone idealists present easy pickings for those who have harder, rougher, judgemental and unforgiving psyches— or who enjoy hunting in packs. Nonetheless, proportionately, more spirits select the idealist attitude during their feline phase than during any other phase because of the opportunities it offers to connect with their higher drives and manifest them pragmatically in the world.

To again speak generally, the elephant phase is when spirits seek to connect to their spiritual self, so at this stage of their evolution spirits are more likely to select the spiritualist attitude than that of idealist. There are exceptions, of course, especially among those who are more inclined to action due to the make-up of their core disposition and are correspondingly less comfortable with too much inwardness. These are the ones who criticise others for doing too much navel-gazing, so for them to usefully connect to their spiritual self the more socially-engaged idealist attitude may be a more appropriate fit than the experiential spiritualist attitude. For these individuals, the idealist attitude is used as a psychological stepping stone to prepare their inward ground for more personally demanding spiritual activities.

SCEPTIC

Some people, discomforted by introspection, view scepticism as a kind of "evil twin" of idealism. Truth be told, such people are probably not wild about idealism, either. This is especially so among those who have adopted realist and pragmatic attitudes. They can't see why anyone would devote so much effort to sceptical nit-picking, particularly with respect to things that they feel cannot or should not be changed. In practice, the sceptic performs a function in human culture that is as essential as that of the idealist.

As noted earlier, the sceptic and idealist are paired. In broad terms, the difference between them is that the first is more internally directed and the second more outwardly directed. What they share is that they are variations on the one underlying approach to life, that being to challenge the status quo and spur everyone to a higher level of functioning. The sceptic tends to be the one who digs deeper and explores the issues with great tenacity whereas the idealist focuses more on getting things happening. Yet these are interdependent activities, with the idealist needing to be sufficiently sceptical to investigate what is going on and not be naïve in his or her approach, and the sceptic needing at least a pinch of idealism to balance the negative responses that are often stirred by what is discovered and to stay motivated to keep digging. The positivity of being idealistic is necessary because otherwise those sceptics whose everyday awareness is dominated by false personality may find their sceptical perceptions start devouring them psychologically, and they end up being eternally suspicious, judging others negatively or always expecting the worst—because if you look for the worst you will certainly find it, given the ways human beings treat others and exploit the world around them.

Those in their field mouse phase mostly find the sceptic attitude too intense to handle and so avoid it. The exception is among those who are willing to use their intellect to provide some psychological balance in their life. Using their intellect to establish balance is a tall order for most people, let alone anyone still in the mouse phase, but it does happen, especially among those who are comfortable with intellectual functioning. The way the sceptic attitude promotes psychological balance is that it provides a questioning trait that holds back the sub-personality from reacting to life circumstances. As a result it isn't swamped by daily life experiences. This is a relief because feeling swamped is a common sensation during the field mouse phase. We have already mentioned that some use threatening and violent behaviour as a way to hold people at bay and so disrupt the feeling of being swamped. Being threatening and violent are emotional and physical solutions. Being sceptical is an intellectual solution to the same experiential conundrum of counteracting the swamped feeling.

For those in the grasshopper phase, the sceptic attitude is adopted for the same reason as the idealist attitude: it adds spice to the life journey. It is also usually put into practice within a group context, which provides safety in numbers and so helps individuals maintain a sense of being in balance and that life circumstances are controlled. In this sense, the sceptical attitude extends the work done during the field mouse phase, supporting the development of the trait of detachment while simultaneously helping the spirit dig deeper into what is happening around it.

Scepticism may be seen to be a necessary foundation for the self-actualising trait of realism, which, like idealism, involves the active application of what is perceived. Some spirits may shift back and forth between the sceptical and realist attitudes over a series of lives to build up their critical faculties. The sceptical attitude also lays down psychological foundations that facilitate self-transformation. During the grasshopper stage individual spirits tend to jump from one experience to another, so from time to time they need need time-out to catch their breath—we're referring to a time-out lasting a lifetime, not just weeks or months. They use this extended period to digest what they have undergone. The sceptical attitude in conjunction with an orientation of repression may be adopted to sustain an extended bout of introspection. Success will depend on the degree to which the individual is able to connect with their essence level drives and perceive and critique themselves. If the false personality dominates the everyday awareness, negative traits such as self-pity, resentment or depression may interfere with the required self-critiquing and derail the process. For this reason, during the grasshopper phase most self-critiquing occurs between lives. Only during the feline phase do individuals tend to have sufficient experiential stock to self-critique without unbalancing their sub-personality's psychology.

During the feline phase, the sceptic attitude is generally adopted to facilitate the development of a variety of traits related to introspection. Only a small minority of spirits have a core disposition that inclines them to really enjoy introspecting and analysing the world around them—we distinguish introspection, which involves sustained focused thinking, from spiritual meditation, in which the absence of thought is promoted. Ironically, more individuals end up being more comfortable with intense silence than intense thought. We say this is ironic because most people would likely think the opposite. Certainly, people have a lot of thoughts passing automatically and incessantly through their minds, but as spirits mature by virtue of passing through their incarnational phases, most find that interrupting the flow of thoughts and thinking in a focused manner is more difficult than interrupting the flow and not thinking at all. We note this is only the case when spirits are incarnated, not when they are in a discarnated state. Accordingly, during the feline stage the sceptic attitude could be adopted in conjunction with other aligned traits as a kind of shock tactic, to force the sub-personality to confront what it is doing. In this situation the sceptical attitude is a psychological tool used to help deepen perceptions. It is usually adopted over a number of lives, often with breaks, in order to learn to be perceptive as well as positively critical. A series of lives is necessary because it takes considerable effort to bed-in these traits at the deep essence level.

During the elephant phase, the sceptical attitude is one of a number of psychological tools available to facilitate self-transformation. Its adoption depends on what the individual has or hasn't faced up to during its feline phase. If karmic issues have not been addressed, inwardly directed scepticism brings individuals face-to-face with their shortcomings. There is one other reason the sceptic attitude might be adopted during this final phase. It might be to help others. By this time individuals have worked through a great deal of their own negative and limiting behaviours, so they may adopt the sceptical attitude, which they socially share, to help others face up to their own limitations. A philosopher like Socrates did this in ancient Athens, bringing his fellow citizens face-to-face with their shortcomings. While he was executed for his trouble, over two thousand years later his deep questioning approach is still known as the Socratic method and his saying, "An unexamined life is not worth living," remains axiomatic for many.

PRAGMATIST

The pragmatist attitude is the simplest of the seven attitudes. Like the other self-neutralising traits, it is chosen because it can have minimal impact on an individual's psychology, allowing other traits to come to the fore.

The pragmatist attitude involves being practical, but exactly how this manifests depends on what other traits are present and what kinds of life experience the individual's accumulated human identity possesses. The pragmatist attitude is similar to the self-actualising realist and cynic attitudes in that it focuses on immediate life situations. But pragmatists are less active in their response than realists and less interrogative than cynics. This means that pragmatists do not naturally have the same depth and all-round perception possessed by realists and cynics—although prior experience has a marked impact on any personality's depth and breadth of perception, and other traits encourage or diminish an intent to peer "behind" things. This means that, in general, the pragmatist attitude promotes immediate and shallow perceptions and passive responses. It is this minimalism that allows other traits to come to the fore. It also explains why the pragmatist attitude may be usefully adopted during all four phases of the incarnational cycle.

During the field mouse phase the pragmatist attitude is useful because it helps newly incarnated spirits see what is happening around them, but it doesn't push them to react and engage with what they perceive. Being the least demanding of the attitudes, it is one of the go-to traits adopted by spirits as they acquire human motor, emotional, cognitive and social skills.

During the grasshopper phase the pragmatist attitude is useful for the same reason, because when new fields of human endeavour and new traits are being tried out, adopting the practical pragmatist attitude helps individuals keep their sub-personalities grounded in life situations. Few people enjoy being surprised, whether by unexpected life circumstances or by un-anticipated inner reactions, given that both can radically alter the course a life takes. Unanticipated inner responses occur when deep essence traits unexpectedly "pop out" into the everyday awareness and impact on what individuals think they are doing. Often these "pop outs" are brief and are explained away on the grounds that they are out-of-character moments. This explanation is accepted because the out-of-character moments usually flare up and die away quickly, and because they rarely lead to an individual alter-ing the course of their life completely—although that can happen.

Of course, this explanation is wrong. Such out-of-character moments are actually completely in-character. How so? Because they involve traits fostered by an individual spirit's sub-personalities during prior lives. When each sub-personality dies, the traits it has fostered are uploaded to the deep essence store within the spirit's accumulated human identity. During a later life, circumstances then trigger a deep psychological response, the result of which is that the trait then "pops out" and generates the supposedly out-of-character moment. In fact, no psychological reactions ever come from no-where, and such moments actually offer a very useful insight into a particu-lar aspect of an individual's deep essence make-up.

To return to our consideration of the pragmatist attitude, its shallow fo-cus dampens inner reactions and so softens the impact of external and inter-nal stimuli, especially intense stimuli that would likely rock those who have adopted any of the other six attitudes. Straightforward practical pragmatism helps individuals get on with their life without becoming bogged down in nuanced feelings and thoughts. This is useful during the grasshopper phase when a range of almost random experiences are undertaken and the incar-nating spirit finds the stability the pragmatist attitude provides helpful in negotiating new and usually challenging situations. The other six attitudes often generate demands of their own in the group situations those in the grasshopper phase prefer, complicating relationships and tasks. Simple prag-matism makes it easier for an individual to go along with what everyone else in the group is doing. In general, the grasshopper pragmatist doesn't rock the boat. For this reason the pragmatist attitude is something of a go-to trait for those in their grasshopper phase, most commonly adopted to help the sub-personality steer a steady course through life.

During the feline phase spirits are more deliberate in their choices, so when the pragmatist attitude is adopted it is usually to help the individual achieve specific goals. The field mouse phase is about learning basic skills, the grasshopper phase is about testing oneself in a range of experiences and using those experiences to develop skills into abilities and talents, and the feline phase is about developing abilities and talents to achieve high levels of performance. It is also about extending perceptions, growing understanding, and learning to negotiate complex situations, not just with minimal fuss, but with keenness and poise. During the feline phase spirits set themselves specific challenges and often grapple with complex situations, using them to grow the experiential store of their accumulated human identity, which directly contributes to their evolution as a spiritual identity. Because by the feline phase spirits have experienced numerous different human situations and have taken on all kinds of roles, and because experience has helped them develop an appreciation of what they enjoy and wish to develop and what they don't wish to develop and would rather stay away from, this phase is when spirits do the most work to develop the inclinations present deep in their core disposition. The passive pragmatist attitude usefully contributes to this development when the spirit has decided other essence traits need to dominate their sub-personality, or when abilities developed in prior lives are being bedded-in and a simple practical attitude helps do so.

Those in the elephant phase are involved in addressing and resolving complex karmic and relationship ties. As they approach the end of their cycle these ties are straightened out and individuals increasingly prefer simplicity in their life situations. For this reason the pragmatist attitude appeals during this phase and is frequently adopted. In this preference for simple practicality they mirror those in the field mouse phase, but of course there is a vast difference between the two phases, because while the elephants are simple in terms of how they live their life, this simplicity is deceptive given the great depth of their experiential stores.

For the observant, simplicity in an individual who otherwise appears to be what is colloquially known as an old soul is a mark of someone who is nearing the end of their incarnation cycle. This preference for simplicity is much misunderstood, especially by those in the grasshopper and feline phases who are attracted to excitement and complexity respectively, and who therefore think, using their own preferences as a standard against which to measure everyone else's behaviour, that excitement and complexity define a successful life. As we keep reiterating, success actually depends on the context in which a life is being lived and what the individual living it is striving to achieve.

The negative aspect of the pragmatist attitude manifests in dogmatism. Practicality requires being open to immediate stimulus and going with the group flow. However, when a sub-personality is closed down by fears it becomes self-defensive, and instead of being practical it becomes dogmatic. Specific dogmas are adopted from the immediate social environment, or in the case of more experienced individuals may involve an outlook of their own devising that others perceive as quirky or cranky. In times past, publicly pronounced dogma was predominantly religious. Today many pragmatists take refuge in economic dogma and in various kinds of rationalistic formulas. Few people are as dangerous as domineering or coercive personalities who use pragmatism as a rationale for instituting suffocating social policies or to control the fates of others. It is educative to consider why so many people go along with these domineering and coercive personalities. The vast majority of human beings have adopted the pragmatic attitude many times during their prior lives. As a consequence, pragmatic behaviour has been uploaded to almost everyone's accumulated human identity, and so almost all human beings can readily appreciate the value of being pragmatic and practical in life. This is why public appeals to being pragmatic receive little objection, even when those appeals are made by domineering and coercive individuals, and when their appeals are clearly dogmatic rather than practical, and closed and grounded in fear rather than openly negotiating with life circumstances. It is this common, almost automatic, acceptance that makes scoundrel personalities who use pragmatism dogmatically so dangerous.

This widespread familiarity with pragmatism also explains a converse situation. Where appeals to pragmatism are generally readily accepted by the wider populace, this is not the case with similar kinds of public appeals made by spiritualists and idealists, who are calling on humanity's higher inner experiences and understanding. The simple explanation for this dispar-ity is that fewer human beings have repeatedly adopted the spiritualist and idealist attitudes, which means only a minority of the total human populace have uploaded spiritual and idealist experiences and behaviours to their ac-cumulated human identity. As a result, far fewer people are comfortable with their own higher impulses, so appeals made to the higher impulses of the world population fall on deaf ears. This situation will change as more in-carnating spirits enter the latter half of their feline phase and their elephant phase. Until then, the majority will find appeals to their higher impulses challenging, simply because they don't know what they are. In the meantime, simplistic dogmatic calls to be practical will win out.

HOW TO UNDERSTAND ATTITUDES

What we are attempting to make clear here is that any single psychological trait is part of a collection of traits. We make three points regarding this.

For you to appreciate how a trait manifests psychologically, it is neces-sary to appreciate what the other key traits are that sit beside it, and how they alter that trait's functioning. This is the first level of collectivity.

The second level of collectivity is in your accumulated human identity. The specific way any particular psychological trait manifests is impacted by the experiences you had while living with that trait during previous lives. Some individuals are more adroit at working with a particular trait because they have literally lived more years with it and so have had more practice handling it. Other individuals manifest the same trait naïvely because they have lived with it for fewer years. The situations in which they have utilised it have likely not been complex, so they are still getting to grips with how it manifests within their overall behaviour and are still learning how to in-tegrate it into their other key traits. Their naïvety results from not having explored a wide range of different situations while in possession of that trait, and so not yet having experienced the different ways the trait can manifest within their accumulating psyche. As they gain more experience they will progressively come to grips with the behavioural and relational nuances each trait involves.

These two levels of collectivity—their general interactivity with other traits, and how your traits function within your accumulated human identity—apply to all traits. In the case of attitude, a third level of collectivity also applies. This is at the level of the essence self, because life goal, orientation and attitude work together to provide the key psychological factors that drive each individual sub-personality as it pursues its life journey. Attitude at this level requires multiple levels of evaluation.

- First you need to identify which attitude you have chosen.
- Then you need to investigate how it functions within your personality. What particular life situations does it steer you into or away from? Self-observation will reveal a pattern. What are your attitude's nuances? Is it a powerful driver or does it take a back seat within your essence self? Does it bring up feelings of frustration or satisfaction or something else? If so, why?
- Some of the answers to these questions will be found when you place your attitude within the triad of life goal and orientation. How does your attitude contribute to the functioning of the other two? Does it work against them? If so, how? What is the overall impact in terms of your daily behaviour?

Having one essence trait working *against* another is not necessarily a bad thing. You may have chosen an attitude that dampens a more fiery orientation, for example, stoicism to calm an orientation of aggression or power or passion. You may have adopted an idealist attitude to enliven a more passively manifesting orientation such as caution. Or you may have selected the realist attitude to temper a life goal of growth, because at the level of your spiritual self you know from experience that the growth life goal tends to manifest in your sub-personalities overly energetically and sometimes intemperately. In this situation, selecting the realist attitude helps the new sub-personality acknowledge life circumstances and be realistic in what it attempts.

We appreciate that analysing the human psychological make-up in this way is not for everyone. We also well know that those who do not analyse themselves miss out on a great deal during their life. Many people agonise for years over their life situations, wondering what they could have done differently, or they carry guilt or regret for decades, all because they don't understand the personality traits that have driven them to do this and not that. A weekend of introspection can resolve a lifetime of agony.

We also appreciate that everyone has to go through what they go through. You who are stimulated by this series of books, and especially those who have reached this page, are most likely in the mid to late sequence in the feline phase or in the elephant phase of your incarnational cycle. This is when individuals begin investigating the nature of their existence to any depth.

We do not state this in order to initiate in you a bout of self-congratulation, that you are doing something others are not. Quite the opposite. We do so to warn you. Delving into your inner make-up will help you connect to your higher capacities and initiate stupendous experiences involving your spiritual self and what lies beyond. You will also be led to confront less savoury aspects of your personality that have their roots in choices and behaviour that occurred during prior incarnations. In order to develop your higher capacities you will have to grapple with traits within your accumulated human personality that are holding you back. Investigating what you have done, in this life and in your many others, will at times cause you to feel profoundly ashamed. As with any journey into unknown places that are challenging to reach, the journey into your layered self involves light and shade, progress and stasis, ecstasy and pain, great ignomy and equally great satisfaction.

Everyday human existence is full of judgement and condemnation. At the spiritual level neither apply. We have experienced all that you are going through now. We understand how difficult incarnation is as a human being. We also know how wonderful it can be. At the level of your own spiritual self you already understand this. While disappointment, regret and shame do exist at the spiritual level, they only occur when individuals evaluate their own performance. All individuals also know deep within that they will have opportunities to correct their errors and perfect traits and abilities. Disappointments are always eventually replaced by success. How fast this occurs depends entirely on how hard you work.

Having identified the key drivers within the essence self, we now need to examine how false personality derails the efforts of the essence self, generating self-disappointment in the first place.

PART FOUR

THE CLASH OF
FALSE AND TRUE

CHAPTER 10

Your Multiple Psychological Momentums

GENERAL STATEMENTS ABOUT REINCARNATION MUST ALWAYS be hedged with qualifications, because they can only be made in relation to specific phases of the overall incarnational cycle. Statements about those in the grasshopper phase generally do not apply to those in the field mouse, feline or elephant phases. In addition, individuals vary. An individual's skills or behaviour may not conform to what is normal during any phase. An individual may depart quite radically from the norm. As a result, before you accept any of our general statements, you need to consider them in relation to the particular people you are striving to understand. Matching a statement to an individual requires a degree of discernment. Without discernment, a general statement may lead you down the proverbial garden path.

Why then make general statements at all, if they need to be qualified, and if they may mislead rather than illuminate? The answer is that general statements have the potential to offer valuable insights into the human situation. Even if they apply only partially—or not at all—if they offer a perspective you hadn't previously considered then they are useful. Accordingly, to begin these chapters on the relationship between what are nominally called true and false personalities we offer some general qualifications.

The chief qualification is that these statements are directed to those in the feline or elephant phases of their cycle. We leave it to you to decide the extent to which our statements apply to yourself and to those you wish to understand. Practise discernment. As is said in the human world when transactions take place, *caveat emptor*: buyer beware.

The reason we are offering general statements in relation to the late feline and the elephant phases is that it is individuals in these phases who are
most likely to be attracted to, and find informative, the perspectives offered
here. Of course, some in the grasshopper phase, and even conceivably in the
field mouse phase, may be sufficiently curious to peruse these words. If they
do they will likely find something of value to them. Nonetheless, and to make
another general statement, it is during the feline and elephant phases that individuals seriously investigate the issues on which we are commenting: the
way a life is structured, why individuals are the way they are, why human
beings behave the way they do, why lives seem so often to go sideways, what
happens before and after a life, and what it all adds up to.

Previous books in this series have broached aspects of these topics. In
this and the next two chapters we will address the issue of why lives go sideways, fall short, or do not deliver on what they are set up to achieve, and how
clashes between what we are nominally calling true and false personalities
are involved in this.

PSYCHOLOGICAL MAKE-UP AS MOMENTUM

At this point we return to the concept of momentum. Previously, we introduced the idea that human identity involves two primary momentums. The
first is the momentum of the essence self as it manifests the desires and aims
of the spiritual self in this life. The second is the momentum of the socialised
self, which is shaped during childhood by biological and social factors.

In the way we wish to discuss psychology here, personality may be
viewed in terms of momentum. True personality is the momentum generated by life goal, orientation and attitude functioning together at the level of
the essence self. False personality is the momentum collectively generated
by fear, chief feature and defensive behaviours functioning at the level of
the socialised self. However, fear, chief feature and defensive behaviours can
also leak into the essence self, shifting essence qualities from their positive to
the negative poles. We'll discuss this in the next chapter.

Of course, every life actually involves multiple momentums. Careers
have their own momentum, as do relationships, marriages, families and per-

sonal development. Economic forces have a momentum that acts externally on citizens' lives. Social tensions provide other kinds of momentum, such as the momentum to outlaw slavery that developed in previous centuries, and the momentum to recognise transgender people at the time of writing this, which follows on a prior social momentum that led to same sex marriage being endorsed in law. These kinds of social momentums are multiple. For now we will ignore them and examine just the momentum behind your psychological make-up.

Ultimately, the momentum of your psychological make-up comes out of your accumulated human identity. We remind you that no one else has put anything into your accumulated human identity. It is entirely your creation. Every skill, ability and talent, each positive and negative trait, every karmic obligation, each piece of knowledge and wisdom, is there because you were attracted to it, you developed it, you honed it. Who you are now, what you are able to do, all your strengths, foibles and weaknesses, are present in your current personality because they are part of your accumulated human identity. Don't conjure up God, or fate, or blame what others have done to you to explain who you are. You are who you are because of what you chose and accomplished in previous lives.

So, at the deepest level, the psychological momentum you have in this life reflects the momentum of your accumulated human identity. Similarly, the essence level traits we discussed previously were selected by you to utilise in this life in the context of the momentum of your accumulated human identity. This leads us to the issue of inertial mass.

PSYCHOLOGICAL MAKE-UP AND INERTIAL MASS

Physics has the principle of inertial mass. Each body has an inertial mass that keeps it moving in its current direction and at its current velocity. Inertial mass is resistant to change. If an object or body is stationary it will continue to be stationary until new energy is supplied to it. If it is already moving, it will continue doing so until its energy is altered, which then changes its direction or velocity, or both.

The same principle applies to your psychological momentum. Psychologically, you possess an inertial mass that continues doing what it does until its energy dissipates or it strikes a difficult situation. Even then, your psychological inertial mass is such that your psyche will attempt to absorb what happens, make minimal adjustment, then carry on as before.

On the one hand, the inertial mass of your psychological make-up is a good thing, because it provides stability. After you go to sleep at night you wake up with the same psychological configuration the next morning. Socially, this is useful, because it results in you being the same person from one day to the next. On the other hand, it is a limitation, because its natural resistance to change makes transforming your psychological make-up a difficult task. Transformation takes sustained effort because you are not changing just one trait but your whole psychological inertial mass.

There is a major implication to this. Once you have lived a few hundred lives your accumulated human identity contains certain dominant traits that give it a specific psychological momentum. So when you complete a life and contemplate what traits you will select for your upcoming lives, you are already working within certain parameters. To return to our metaphor of the boat, your accumulated human identity is already loaded with specific materials, is headed in a certain direction, and possesses a particular velocity. You can deviate a little to this side or that, but to change your psychological load, direction or speed takes application performed over an extended period. Change at a fundamental level can certainly be achieved, but to do so the psychological momentum of your accumulated human identity has to be altered.

MOMENTUM AND GOING OFF PLAN

A question could be asked at this point. Earlier we noted that individuals can choose to go off their life plan. Aren't we now contradicting that statement? If human psychology follows its inertial momentum, how is it possible to make *any* kind of radical choice? How can anyone *really* depart from their life plan?

The answer is that no one has just one psychological momentum. The overall momentum of your accumulated human identity is made up of numerous momentums. For example, your development of a particular talent has one momentum. Each goal you set yourself has its momentum. Your relationships with other spiritual identities, with whom you regularly incarnate, have their own momentums. Most human spiritual identities have dozens of such relationships, so there are multiple relationship momentums within each accumulated identity.

Each of your traits also has its own momentum. Some traits, for example the attitude of scepticism, you may be introducing into your psychological make-up for the first time, in which case you'll still be grappling with how to apply it. Another trait, such as the passion orientation, you may have adopted many times before so you have learned how to keep it in balance with your other traits. Accordingly, different psychological traits have been experienced in different contexts, have different levels of development, and are at different levels of integration. They each have their differing momentums. As a result, when individuals go off plan, what they choose to do instead is selected in the context of what appeals to them in relation to some other aspect of their accumulated human identity. That is, their choice is made in the context of other momentums already existing deep within them.

It is not possible to incorporate all the momentums present within your accumulated human identity in a single life. Your accumulated human identity is too complex. It contains too much. In addition, some abilities and traits contradict others, at least within a human context. So when planning a life you always have to select related factors from your accumulated life experience and ignore others. The plan may be to live a sedate family life as a responsible husband or wife. But then the choice is made during the life to ditch that plan and run away with a lover, or take up a new work opportunity, or pursue an offer of adventure. All these are real possibilities only because they appeal to momentums that already exist within the individual's accumulated human identity. So the choice to go off plan is not made arbitrarily. Nor are alternative life choices made arbitrarily. This means that going off plan can be described as choosing to jump from one momentum to another, to respond to the attraction of one aspect of the full accumulated psychological inertial mass over another aspect.

Remember, however, that radical changes in a life may also be part of a life plan. The woman who leaves her husband and children may be doing so in accordance with the life plans of everyone involved. In fact, this is very likely the case. Only in a very small number of lives do individuals go significantly off plan. Their psychological momentum prevents them from doing so.

FALSE PERSONALITY AND LOSING MOMENTUM

To return to our discussion of psychological momentum, no one's life momentum is optimal. By that we mean no one is implementing every single aspect of their life plan to its maximum potential. We don't say this to deflate you. Far from it. We say it because the fact is that no one lives their life without at least some negative impact from false personality.

We have just commented on how people may depart from their life plan to engage with other goals. This happens, but is not common. By far the most common reason people depart from their life plan is because they are negatively influenced by their false personality. By "departure from their life plan" we don't mean they ditch what they are doing and take up some other significant task. Rather, they depart from their life plan insofar as they don't implement it, whether in part or majorly. So what we are describing here is not a situation in which the ship of your essence self changes direction, and instead of steaming towards your planned next port of call it heads somewhere else. Rather, what we mean is that the ship of your essence self either travels much more slowly than planned, or doesn't leave port at all. It doesn't go anywhere. It doesn't set other goals for itself, it remains as is, where is. Its momentum is impeded. It is no longer focused on developing its skills, abilities and talents. Stasis is the most common negative impact that false personality has on the momentum of the essence self.

As we stated, no one is free of at least some of the negative impacts false personality has on their life progress. Everyone has experienced times when fear, or lack of confidence, or over-confidence, or second-guesssing, or defensiveness, or any of many other traits, caused them to hesitate and not do what deep down they wanted to do. This is how false personality causes you to depart from your life plan—not by offering you an equally compelling new goal, but by stopping you making progress at all. As this is a significant issue, we will examine it in more detail.

CHAPTER 11

How False Personality
Hijacks the Essence Self

TO BEGIN THIS DISCUSSION OF HOW FALSE PERSONALITY STOPS
you from achieving parts of your life plan, let's summarise your life situation. You are born into a body that has certain genetic predispositions. The family and social environment in which you are raised imposes specific attitudes, beliefs, and behaviours on you. Because human existence is complex and difficult, you develop defensive behaviours to help you cope with trying situations. These self-defensive behaviours are gathered around a chief feature that has a specific fear at its core. Over time these fear-based self-defensive traits become imbedded in your socialised self.

You also have an essence self. Your essence self is an expression of your spiritual self. It is the higher human part of you that is seeking to fulfil specific tasks, develop skills, foster abilities, and express talents. It is the best of your human sub-personality this time round. But in order to function in the world, in order for you to work with other people, your essence self has to express itself via your socialised self. By the time you reach adulthood you have achieved a functioning balance between your socialised self and your essence self.

Your socialised self possesses a number of neutral traits that enable you to interact effectively with others: language, customs, socially agreed ways of behaving. But it also has a dark side, consisting of your deep fears, your chief feature, and buried defensive attitudes. Collectively, these dark aspects of your socialised self are inhibitory mechanisms that slow or even halt completely what your essence self is trying to achieve. We are calling these fear-centered, self-defensive, inhibitory traits false personality. Psychologically, they have their own momentum within you, their own inertial mass. And this momentum leaks into and impacts on the growth of your essence self. This is what we will now discuss.

AWARENESS AND EVERYDAY FOCUS

Everyday awareness is malleable. It is capable of jumping from one activity to another in the blink of an eye. Confirmation of this fact is found when you remember the occasions when you began one task then found yourself doing another. Or when you start thinking about one topic and discover that your mind has switched to something else, but you made no conscious decision to make the shift. It occurred without your conscious involvement.

Everyday awareness is actually easily captured and diverted. It is like a cork floating on the ocean. When the tide flows, it moves in that direction, then when a boat motors past it is caught in the wake and bobs in the new direction. Wherever the surface flows goes, the cork goes with it. This is similar to what happens to your everyday awareness. It gets caught up in whatever is happening around it and it goes with the flow of that activity. On one level this is understandable, because attachment and identification are part and parcel of human life. They glue you to the daily existence that you signed up for. However, there is a deeper level to this process.

Everyday awareness is also very much impacted by inner tides. We are referring here to psychological momentums. As we made clear in the previous chapter, each person has multiple momentums flowing through their layered self. The momentums that inwardly dominate most people consist of biological momentums, which are instinctual in nature, and psychological momentums that function at the levels of the socialised and essence selves. These act in concert with momentums existing in the external world to create an inner-outer synergy.

By the phrase "inner-outer synergy" we refer to the fact that the specific momentums in the exterior world that individuals latch onto are attractive because they resonate with an individual's inner impulses and traits. Thus your inner traits, your inner predilections, lead you to reach out to and latch onto particular people, objects and events. At the same time you ignore other people, objects and events that are equally available to you. Why? Because they don't resonate with you. That is, they don't resonate with the instinctual and psychological momentums that, at that particular moment, are dominant within you. In this way the attachments and identifications that keep you engaged with the activities of daily life are the result of inner-outer synergy. Take away the synergy, as happens when people suffer a traumatic shock or are given antipsychotic drugs, and individuals become limp and unresponsive. This indicates the power of inner-outer synergy, as well as the extent to which it dominates human interactions; indeed, it could be argued, the extent to which it makes those interactions possible at all.

While all this is happening, your everyday awareness is like a cork. It is there for the ride. As the balance of your inner-outer synergy shifts, as one momentum surges up to dominate, so your awareness goes with it. And as another surges up to replace it, or as a new stimulus impacts on your body from outside you, so your awareness bobs around to follow it.

This would all be a neutral, albeit frustrating, facet of human existence if this was all that is involved. It would be neutral if all momentums were equal, and frustrating because if all momentums were equal your awareness would never settle, being taken first this way, then that way, then in yet another direction, depending on what inner surge or outward event was dominant moment by moment during the course of a day. But the situation is not neutral. The fact is, the inner-outer synergy is dominated by two particular momentums among them all. These are the momentums we have labelled true personality and false personality.

The traits present in true personality give you focus. They enable you to hone in on particular aspects of life, select certain people, objects and events from the myriads available, and keep your everyday awareness focused on those above everything else. This is the upside. The downside is that the false personality's traits, present in the form of fear, chief feature and limiting behaviours, interrupt the essence self's focus and divert it away from achieving its goals. When this happens it can be said that false personality has leaked into true personality, taking it into its negative poles.

HOW THE ESSENCE SELF IS HIJACKED

We have previously outlined how the essence self's momentum results from the combination of life goal, orientation and attitude. The combination of these three characteristics, augmented by other attributes drawn from the accumulated human identity—including deep essence qualities, personally developed abilities and traits, and karmic obligations— gives each individual a unique essence level identity and momentum.

At this point we need to clarify our perspective. We are asserting that individuals are functioning in concert with their true personality when the positive poles of their essence self are engaged. Alternatively, they are functioning in concert with their false personality when the negative poles of their essence self are engaged. For the sake of simplicity, we will initially describe this dichotomy in relation to just life goal, orientation and attitude. We will then widen, and deepen, the analysis.

In the previous chapters on life goal, orientation and attitude, we discussed both the positive and negative psychological manifestations of the seven characteristics of each. We suggest you return to the relevant chapters and review what is stated there. (Orientations and attitudes are discussed in earlier chapters, life goals in *Practical Spirituality*.) Such a review will obviate the need for us to spend pages repeating here what has already been stated at length there. Assuming you have re-read that material, we now propose to build on our previous statements regarding the negative poles of life goal, orientation and attitude.

When people become fearful and defensive, psychologically they tend to slide into the negative manifestations of their primary essence traits. For example, those with a realist attitude start acting on imagined suppositions rather than real perceptions; those with a cynic attitude judge and denigrate others instead of finding contradictions in what they say or do; the spiritualist shifts from seeking verification and instead surrenders to making and defending statements of faith; and the pragmatist attitude abandons being practical in favour of being dogmatic. The same pattern is repeated in the case of orientation and life goal. As a handy reminder for you, and to aid our explanation, we have asked our scribe to reinsert the relevant graphics here.

As you examine each of the three graphics, you will observe that there are twenty-one negative poles of psychological outlook and behaviour. Some will be primary for you in your current life, depending on which is your lead attitude, orientation and life goal. Those that dominate your essence level psychological make-up will do so both positively and negatively. As we observed when introducing these traits, some additionally slide into a paired companion. Caution and power provide one such pair, with one being primary and the other possibly becoming active in a secondary role. This sliding between pairs varies according to individual make-up. When sliding does occur, these secondary traits provide a minor undercurrent, which, again depending on circumstances, will itself swing between its positive and negative poles. So you can see that even though you have present in your essence psychological make-up only three of the twenty-one attitudes, orientations and life goals, they may be augmented by others, adding layers to your essence level functioning. We never promised that untangling your psychological make-up would be easy!

It is the reactivity of your false personality that causes you to veer into the negative poles of your three primary essence traits and their secondary un-

THE SEVEN ATTITUDES

	(+)	(−)
SELF-ACTUALISING		
REALIST	Perception	Supposition
CYNIC	Contradiction	Denigration
SELF-TRANSFORMING		
SRIRITUALIST	Verification	Faith
STOIC	Tranquility	Resignation
SELF-FULFILLING		
IDEALIST	Coalesence	Abstraction
SCEPTIC	Investigation	Suspicion
SELF-NEUTRALISING		
PRAGMATIST	Practicality	Dogma

THE SEVEN ORIENTATIONS

	(+)	(−)
SELF-ACTUALISING		
AGGRESSION	Dynamism	Belligerence
PERSEVERANCE	Persistence	Immutability
SELF-TRANSFORMING		
POWER	Authority	Oppression
CAUTION	Deliberation	Procrastination
SELF-FULFILLING		
PASSION	Self-actualisation	Identification
REPRESSION	Restraint	Inhibition
SELF-NEUTRALISING		
OBSERVATION	Clarity	Surveillance

THE SEVEN LIFE GOALS

	(+)	(−)
SELF-ACTUALISING		
DOMINANCE	Leadership	Dictatorship
SUBMISSION	Devotion	Subservience
SELF-TRANSFORMING		
GROWTH	Comprehension	Confusion
REVALUATION	Simplification	Withdrawal
SELF-FULFILLING		
ACCEPTANCE	Agape	Ingratiation
REJECTION	Discrimination	Prejudice
SELF-NEUTRALISING		
EQUILIBRIUM	Suspension	Interia

dercurrents. When something happens to you that you interpret as threatening and so requires you to defend yourself, the behaviours gathered around your chief feature automatically kick in and you respond accordingly. For some the response is to withdraw, for others it involves attacking, either physically or by giving a verbal spray, yet others prefer to deflect away from themselves by making excuses, offering justifications, blaming others, and so on.

We have described this reactive process at length elsewhere. At one point we even described people's defensive reactions as generating "another ugly day on Earth". This is true as far as it does. What we want to do now is to go a little deeper in our analysis, because such defensive behaviour isn't just ugly, it interrupts the momentum of your essence self. It does so when it captures your awareness and shifts your behaviour into its negative poles. This not only puts you into a negative psychological state, it interrupts your essence level functioning. Let's be specific.

In reaction to a jarring external input: (1) your chief feature and its negative defensive traits become active; (2) feelings, thoughts and actions associated with the jarring input fill your awareness; and (3) your everyday self becomes identified with those thoughts, feelings and actions. The false personality is in full cry. Your essence self's momentum is temporarily interrupted. If you identify with your reactive self for an extended period, the essence self's momentum may even be completely halted. In broad terms, false personality centred in your socialised self has activated your psychological defensive traits, resulting in your essence self becoming saturated by the false personality's energy. False personality has hijacked true personality.

You can see this occurring during the times when you get depressed, when you feel things are hopeless, when you wonder why you are bothering, or when you doubt yourself and others. When such feelings and thoughts flood your awareness, the momentum of your essence self is halted and you slump into inner stasis. Be assured that at such times these feelings are emanating from your false personality. This is irrefutably so when they persist for an extended period of time.

As an aside, we note that there are times when an interruption to an individual's life momentum is the result of a turning point being reached, which leads to an individual reappraising who they are and where they are going. They use the turning point to turn their life around. That is not what we are referring to here, because when people become so unhappy or depressed that they reappraise what they are doing and make fundamental life changes, they are acting to facilitate their life plan. They are not in stasis. In contrast, what we are discussing here is when a life becomes paralysed, change is perceived as impossible, and individuals feel stuck as a result of repeatedly engaging with a narrow band of negative feelings, thoughts and actions. Far from fulfilling their life plan, this situation stops them from pursuing their life plan. Such an individual's life is in stasis, stuck in the same repeating psychological states.

For the majority of people it is mostly external events that trigger their slide into inner negativity and stasis. To put this in everyday terms, let's say you experience rejection, whether at work or personally. Usually such rejection is at the level of, and is experienced by you at, the level of your socialised self. At this level rejection triggers the chief feature's crystallised self-defensiveness, which spurs your false personality into action as it reacts in the ways it has developed over the years. But if you also experience the rejection at the level of the essence self, by which we mean if your essence self was involved in the endeavour which has been rejected, then when false personality reacts its negative energy leaks into your attitude, orientation and life goal, which consequently shift into their negative manifestations.

What happens next? Nothing happens. By which we mean, of course you will feel a lot, churning over what has happened in your head and guts, but your essence self's momentum will be interrupted. Your awareness being fully immersed in negative defensive feelings, thoughts and actions, little to no energy is available to be directed into fulfilling your essence self's aims. The essence self's momentum is halted. Stasis sets in.

This, then, describes what happens inside you when an inhibiting stimulus arrives from outside, triggers a defensive response, and the false personality's negative energy washes into your essence self. However, there is another instance in which the momentum of the essence self is interrupted. This is when the inhibiting stimulus comes from within.

WHEN THE INNER POLE DOMINATES

What we have just discussed regarding what happens when an external shock sends the socialised self into self-defensive mode can also be described in terms of inner-outer synergy. Your psychological make-up includes a collection of feelings, thoughts, attitudes and behaviours crystallised around a chief feature. Every chief feature has a specific fear at its core. This, then, makes up a major inner component of your inner-outer synergy. So when an outer event occurs that unsettles you, what happens psychologically is the event creates a stimulus that leads to a welling up inside you of pre-programmed reactive feelings, thoughts, attitudes and behaviour. While you feel it is you responding, in fact it is your crystallised false personality reacting. As we have just noted, its negative energy then floods the essence self, interrupting its momentum.

False personality and true personality provide the two dominant momentums within you psychologically. Individuals carry their crystallised false personality around with them all the time. This is at the heart of their reactions. So when an external event occurs—whether involving a powerful physical interaction, a full-on verbal spray, a glancing word, or even a single look—that event becomes input that is interpreted by the crystallised false personality as a threat. It then reacts in its pre-programmed ways. To put this is everyday terms, everyone has met a person who is known to have a hair-trigger around some issue. You might have observed in yourself situations or people that rub you the wrong way and ignite an instant reactive response. Certain reactive behaviours are often present right on the surface of everyday identity, so it takes only one word, or a mere hint of a particular attitude, for them to flare up. Perhaps it is around a political cause, or around sex, or bosses, or certain food, or an offensive attitude certain people have that really gets up your nose. When you react instantly to such situations, automatically and without thinking, this is crystallised behaviour in operation.

To be clear about the distinction we are making here, in the previous section we drew attention to when an external stimulus triggers an inner response. This is the outer dominating the inner in the inner-outer synergy. What we are now drawing attention to is when the inner pole dominates the outer. Basically, this means that no matter what the external input, a particular preset reaction occurs. We have just commented on the false personality component of this inner pole. We will now consider deeper reactivity, in which traits present within the essence self inhibit its own momentum.

HOW THE ESSENCE SELF HIJACKS ITSELF

You carry false personality and its hair trigger reactions around with you each and every day. These are at the surface of your inner layers. Complicating the picture is that other reactive behaviours are buried at different levels within your psychological make-up, many at the level of your essence self. Because they are deeper it usually takes a reasonably strong stimulus, repeated over time, to trigger a buried essence level reactive response. Indeed, a reactive response may be so deeply buried that you have no idea it even exists. This is especially the case with behaviours shaped by trauma.

If trauma was experienced in this life, it exists in the basement of the biological, socialised or essence selves. Particularly invasive physical trauma likely exists in the basements of all three. If the trauma occurred in a past life, its impact is present in this life via imported deep essence traits. All trauma is repressed. It is held away from everyday awareness by psychological coping mechanisms. Some coping mechanisms are blatantly self-defensive. Others are more subtle. For example, an individual may justify their powerful reaction to a negative stimulus on the grounds that reacting is a matter of asserting fairness, or of providing a dose of social justice, or that the person whose input they are reacting to is just not a good person. But when responses are automatic the reality is that individuals are reacting according to psychological presets buried within them, presets that exist as coping mechanisms to compensate for trauma.

We are not only referring to trauma that was done to them. It could involve trauma that they rained on others and that they now feel deeply disturbed by. It could be that people who are engaged in fights for social or political justice are doing so to rebalance injustices they themselves perpetrated in previous lives. Of course, karmic debts are often also involved.

As we observed regarding karma, the psychological traits that led to another being infringed need to be addressed when resolving karmic links. The psychological trait exists at the essence level in this life and will be incorporated into attitude, orientation or life goal, and its resolution will be part of the life plan. As such, it will dominate in certain external situations. This is another example of when the inner-outer synergy is dominated by the inner pole.

At this point an illustration of what is being discussed has come into our scribe's mind. This is a Sufi story that goes along the lines of a man being asked what a cafe reminds him of. He replies, food. He is asked what a jealous husband reminds him of. He replies, food. And a classy car? Again his response is food. When asked how these three very different things could all remind him of food, he replies that everything reminds him of food. This is a very simplified example of what we are talking about, of when an inner impulse, an inner momentum, dominates the inner-outer synergy.

A more subtle example is that after surviving situations in which food was short, many come out of the experience with the powerful feeling that food is precious. People have told stories about their relatives who survived the privations of World War Two. As children living long after the war was over they didn't understand why their grandparent urged them to eat food that they didn't like, or to continue eating when they had had sufficient, or forbade them to throw out uneaten food. Their grandparent's wartime experiences formed in them the powerful feeling that waste is wrong. In this wartime situation, a powerful external input traumatised them, moulding their psyche and shaping a reactive response they then carried with them for the rest of their lives. The repeated external stimulus of privation generated a reaction that subsequently became crystallised in them psychologically and as a result dominated all their social reactions to do with food. In other words, this crystallised trait has caused the grandparent to interpret all outer situations involving food from one fixed inner perspective.

To extract the lesson we intend from this example, this illustrates how an initial external stimulus, repeated over time, comes to dominate the individual's psyche to such a degree that it permanently distorts that person's psyche. Years later, when privation has long been absent, the individual continues to behave as if privation was still present. The feeling has crystallised psychologically and so provides a dominant momentum. Again, the inner dominates the outer in the inner-outer synergy.

To return to the Sufi story of the man who said that everything reminds him of food, if the trait is made more subtle then the same principle applies. So if we replace the desire for food with the attitude of cynic, an individual with a cynic attitude views all that happens using that one perspective. Earlier we likened attitude to a boat's prow that parts the waters of life. We also said attitude is a filter, that each person's attitude allows in certain external stimuli and ignores others. Again, this is an example of how an inner trait dominates outer stimuli in the inner-outer synergy. We leave you to examine how this applies in relation to your own essence traits.

THE LAYERED SELF SELECTS EXPERIENCES

It can confidently be said that each individual not only views the world through the lens of their psyche, their psyche also acts as a filter via which each *selects* their experiences. Out of the emporium of possibilities available in the human world, and out of all the inwardly available personal responses to those possibilities, each individual's psyche selects both what they encounter from among all the world's possibilities and how they process what they encounter. This means that human experiences have an outer content and an inner content. Each individual experience involves both. But the quality of experiences vary considerably, due to whether, in the moment, the outer stimulus or the individual's inner psychological response dominates their everyday awareness.

We commented earlier about how everyday awareness is easily attracted by passing external stimulus—and the modern world certainly offers multiple distractions. But in this chapter we are attempting to clarify a much more significant aspect of human psychology, which is that in all serious, long-lived and deep interactions with the world and with others living in it, it is the inner pole of the inner-outer synergy that dominates what people do. It isn't the waves of passing external stimuli that dictate how your life goes, it is your deep-seated, often buried psychological traits that steer the ship of your self through the waters of life.

Human identity is very complex. It contains comparatively shallow but powerful impulses emanating from the biological self; crystallised socially conditioned reactions coming from false personality; deep momentums emanating from the essence self; even deeper momentums emanating from deep essence; and the deepest momentum provided by the spiritual self. These momentums also slide between their positive and negative poles. So when we say that each individual selects their experiences, we are referring to the extremely complex ways that every person draws on the combination of traits present in their layered self to psychologically shape their own life experience. And it all happens spontaneously, in the moment they are experiencing it.

Understanding your self involves digging into these layers, separating them, and seeing how one trait at one level is connected to other traits at other levels. The psyche can be thought of as a multi-layered complex of interwoven traits, some of which manifest as brief surges of impulse and others as long-lived, sometimes almost imperceptible momentums. So while we are distinguishing between the five layers of the self to clarify what is involved, in reality they all overlap and intertwine. None exists in isolation. Traits present in your essence self echo into your socialised self. And visa versa. Abilities present genetically, in your body's cognitive system, facilitate essence level expression. Qualities that drive your false personality are significant to your essence self as it attempts to put into action your spiritual self's life plan.

While the outer pole of your inner-outer synergy involves things that happen accidentally to you, the inner pole contains nothing that is there accidentally. Understanding how this is and what is involved, including the impact of experiences undergone in prior lives, is a challenging task. Even a daunting task. Yet with sustained effort much can be understood. We wish you to have no doubt about this. Furthermore, as a result of understanding what is involved, the sting and hurt of much that impacts negatively on your psyche can be diminished.

By working on those negative aspects you can start to crack the crystallised traits that have shaped false personality. Inner work can initially diminish, then eventually eliminate, their self-limiting activity within you. This is the point of dwelling at such length on the psyche's negative aspects. The goal is to remove whatever is stopping you from putting all aspects of your life plan into place. The ultimate goal is for you to achieve your bliss.

In stating this, we assert that addressing negativities is part of almost everyone's life plan. This returns us to the notion of obstacles.

CHAPTER 12

False Personality, Obstacles and Your Life Plan

IN THE PREVIOUS BOOK IN THIS SERIES WE DESCRIBED WHAT happens in your psyche as a war between the momentum of your crystallised socialised self, driven by its self-defensiveness and fears, and the momentum of your essence self, steered psychologically by its life goal as it seeks to accomplish the tasks incorporated into your spiritual self's life plan. In this book we have extended on what is involved by saying that the war may be viewed as being between the momentums of false personality and true personality. We have provided detailed material on the false and true personalities, noting that they consist of a complex combination of competing, aligned and sliding traits. At the level of your everyday awareness there is indeed a war, with each momentum battling for your time, energy and attention. But at the level of your spiritualised self it is not a war. It is all part of your life plan.

It is easy to demonise false personality. It is easy to label it as a devil that is wrecking your life. This labelling is derived from the religious attitude that conceives of the Devil as challenging God by interceding in human lives and leading souls astray. In the same way, it is possible to assume that false personality acts in opposition to your true personality, interceding in daily life and leading you astray. This is not the case. Projecting antique religious notions onto true and false personality creates a false dichotomy. This kind of judgement neither accurately reflects their respective roles in your life, nor does it truly describe their relationship to each other.

Rather than seeing true and false personality as a dichotomy, we return to the concept of synergy. True and false personality exist together in an interlaced relationship in order to facilitate the fulfilment of your life plan. While we have already said much about this, nonetheless we'll unpack this statement a little more.

USING OBSTACLE TRAITS

To get this discussion under way we will utilise an example drawn from everyday life. The example is of a knife blade, which is sharpened by the process of abrasion against a whetstone. By being drawn across the whetstone's hard resisting surface, the blade's dull edge is worn away and the blade becomes sharp. Similarly, an individual psyche is "sharpened" through abrasion, that is, by being rubbed against opposed psychological qualities. In the context of this discussion, the knife and whetstone represent true and false personality. To explain how the process works we will explore the example of an individual possessing a talent that requires further development.

We have previously discussed the fact that no skill or talent exists in pristine isolation within your psyche. Other traits are necessarily attached to it. This is because in previous lives, as you developed a particular talent, it was done in a specific social environment. That social environment engendered a range of emotional responses in you. These perhaps included self-doubt, frustration, fear of rejection, feelings engendered by actually being rejected, jealousy that others' talents were being more recognised than yours, arrogance in response to praise, and satisfaction that your talent was being expressed. If in another life you continued building on that talent, then new related social circumstances would have stimulated new positive and negative responses within you. This would be repeated as you continued to develop your talent over a dozen or more lifetimes.

It means that by the time you reach the mature phase of your incarnational cycle, you will have a number of positive and negative psychological traits present in your accumulated human identity that exist in relation to that particular talent. When you incorporate that talent in a new life, at least some of all those associated negative and positive traits will be brought into the life too, to be worked on in tandem with the talent. As we have described in *Practical Spirituality*, the family situation and the social environment you choose to be born into stimulate in you certain positive and negative traits. Positive essence level traits will contribute to your true personality, while the negative traits will end up crystallised into false personality. Clearly, this is not a negative scenario. It is very positive.

In effect, it means that negative traits become obstacles that, by their nature, inhibit the expression of your talent. However, when you face up to and address those negative traits, when you work to replace them with positive, self-nurturing traits, you are not only overcoming the negativities, you are also further developing your talent, enabling you to utilise it effectively in a wide variety of situations, including those that are challenging or even working in a contrary direction to what you are striving to achieve. In this way you develop essence level strength. In terms of inner-outer synergy, you learn to deliberately and consciously hold to an inner momentum, no matter what happens to you, and in spite of prevailing external conditions.

Therefore, just as you sharpen the knife blade by rubbing it on a stone, so you develop your skills and talents by "rubbing" them against your own negative traits. In this way false personality isn't devilish at all, but rather provides a rigid and opposed force which true personality can rub up against as it seeks to perfect its abilities in a diverse range of situations and scenarios.

THE MULTI-LIFE PERSPECTIVE

It has been said that no one is an island. In the context of this discussion, we suggest that a series of lives may be viewed as a string of islands. Each island contains certain creatures and a set of prevailing conditions. For example, one island may be dominated by monkeys and banana trees, each supporting the other synergistically, and another by birds and predatory cats at war with one another. But because the islands exist as a chain, they are linked under the water, and so do not exist in isolation. In effect, they form an archipelago of possibilities.

Let's say there are one hundred islands, standing together in the ocean. Some exist serially, one following another to form a line, some are clumped closely together, and others are dotted at a distance, apparently positioned randomly in relation to the others. Nonetheless, all are interlinked under the water and so are part of one extended archipelago. This is also how a series of one hundred lives exist in relation to each other—remembering, of course, that we are referring here to the lives of maturing individuals who have reached the feline or elephant phases of their incarnational cycles.

If you adopt an overview position, say by flying high above the ocean, you would see the islands are laid out in patterns. This is how a sequence of one hundred lives would also look to you. The islands that are strung out in a more-or-less straight line represent lives that build one on another. You have selected the conditions on each of these islands to aid the sequential development of a range of your essence abilities and traits. The islands that are bunched close to each other represent a series of lives in which you struggled with, and so circled around, a particular set of traits, or needed repeated efforts to develop a particular ability or talent. Conditions on these islands are similar because these lives drew on related aspects of your accumulated human identity, as you adjusted them from one life to the next in order to eventually achieve the optimal performance of what you were working on. The oddly dotted islands, some distance from all the others, represent traits and abilities that you have been tidying up. The conditions in these lives actually relate to issues and situations from distant prior lives, lived long before your current one hundred life sequence. You choose to have these lives because, having developed new inner resources, you can now address and more easily resolve issues from those distant lives in just a life or two.

Each island has a life plan governing it. On each you choose certain positive and negative conditions to prevail. These conditions reflect traits present in your socialised and essence selves that manifest in what we have nominally called your false and true personalities. Related positive and negative traits are selected in tandem so you may hone your inner resources, so you may "sharpen your blade". Life plans change from life to life as you progressively achieve the inner and outer goals you set yourself. And the underlying purpose is developmental, to enhance the capabilities of your accumulated human identity.

THE USEFULNESS OF A MULTI-LIFE PERSPECTIVE

This is a very simple, even simplistic, picture of what happens as you select from and work with all the multiple momentums existing within your accumulated human identity.

Nonetheless, we offer it because it is useful to stand back and take a longer view of what has shaped your current life. It is easy to become caught up in the pains and pleasures of daily existence and forget that, actually, this life is just one in a series of related lives. The issues you are addressing this time round are not completely new to you. Neither will those you love, nor those you interact with most intensely, be strangers to you. You know one another on the spiritual level and will likely have interacted previously. Similarly, the issues you face now are just one phase of a series of related issues that you are progressively working your way through.

So this life, which seems to be isolated, at least as far as you experience it, is one of a sequence of related lives. By delving into the issues we are illuminating here, by examining your deep nature, you can gain insights into how those talents and traits you now possess came to be present. And you can put both the positive and negative aspects of your life into a wider context. Much frustration and uncertainty can be dissolved as a result of understanding how you came to be who you are.

But understanding is just one step. The next is to change who you are, building on what is positive, and diminishing, even eliminating, the negative traits that prevent you from putting into action everything you planned for this life. That is what we will address in the final section.

PART FIVE

TRANSFORMING
WHO YOU ARE

CHAPTER 13

The Practice of Self-Enquiry

BEFORE WE GO INTO ANY DETAILS REGARDING THE PROCESS OF self-transformation, we need to repeat a point we made earlier. Ordinarily, psychological adjustments are focused on getting people to fit in with the social norms that apply where they live. People with extreme behavioural issues are treated in order that they can function within a community, with functioning viewed in terms of being able to hold down a job, perform it competently, and get on reasonably amicably with others. Treatment to achieve this involves therapy, in the form of talking through issues or, what is much more prevalent today, by way of taking pills that chemically adjust moods and behaviour. So if a person has anxiety attacks, or is unhappy, the goal is to enable that person to function in daily life situations. Sometimes, the therapist will get to the root of whatever is causing the anxiety or emotional difficulties, but often the intention is just to alleviate the symptoms to enable the person to function socially. In these situations medication, whether determined by a professional or self-administered, is applied just so the person can get through the day, the week, the month, the year.

The approach to human psychology that we are advocating here is very different. Our approach is developmental, and our process only focuses on symptoms in order to use them to get to their underlying causes, then address those causes. But in order to do this successfully, it is necessary to have some safety nets in place. Right at the start of this book we evoked the image of Pandora's Box being opened. This is what happens when you delve into the deep aspects of your psychology: memories, attitudes and behaviours, some highly unpleasant, even disturbing, are brought into the harsh light of day. And this is often difficult to deal with.

Another issue is that the transformation of your psychological make-up is difficult to achieve, given (1) chief feature and its fear has crystallised in you by adulthood, (2) your false personality, built on that crystallised fear, has developed its own behavioural momentum, and (3) it is likely that nothing in your daily life requires you to change—in fact, transforming the way you approach life will inevitably disrupt long established patterns of feeling, thinking and behaving. Finally, as we have previously observed, taking a hammer to the crystallised aspects of your identity would be detrimental to your psychological health, potentially destabilising it to the degree that you could go mad.

Given all these factors, it is clear that the kind of psychological transformation we are advocating here is not only *not* required by those around you, there is much inside you on a very personal level that doesn't want to engage in the process, and that will, in fact, try to sabotage it. We don't mean this in the sense that some "evil Dr Jekyll" exists inside you actively working to prevent change. We mean it in the sense that the momentums of your innate fear, your derived chief feature, and the traits that constitute your false personality, have a unified momentum that, whenever you attempt to transform one aspect of your feelings, thoughts and behaviour, will function to divert your attention back onto them and so will inherently act as a drag on your attempts to change and inwardly develop.

Balancing this drag on your inner development is a need to have courage. We discussed this in the previous book of this series. Courage is not often considered in relation to psychospiritual transformation. But being willing to open Pandora's Box and face up to what is inside requires immense courage. On the other hand, once negative traits are directly perceived, they come to be seen as not so scary after all. Nonetheless, releasing memories and feelings, much of it uncomfortable, even traumatic, from the depths of your accumulated human identity, is always a fraught exercise.

That is why we mentioned having safety nets in place before opening anything. Accordingly, that is what we will discuss first.

ESTABLISHING SAFE BOUNDARIES

Psychologically, what we are advocating here is a variety of self-administered psychotherapy. In conventional medical, welfare and psychiatric settings, a therapist is present to guide the patient through the difficult process of confronting past situations—of opening up Pandora's Box—in order to understand what has shaped the patient's psyche, and what therefore needs to be faced up to, then adjusted, in order to facilitate self-transformation. The therapist brings her or his expertise to the situation, providing perspective and balance.

Perspective and balance are needed because delving into key formative situations, many of which, as we just noted, were likely traumatic in some way, is a process that is necessarily freighted with intense feelings. These feelings may include guilt, shame, anger, depression, feelings of inadequacy, or surges of violence. The therapist's wider perspective helps the patient put what is uncovered into context and maintain sufficient inner balance to cope with the intense emotions that necessarily surge up into everyday awareness when the past is confronted. In this way, the therapist functions as a safety net, helping prevent the patient from being so overwhelmed by intense emotions that he or she spins off into psychological meltdown.

Accordingly, before engaging in self-administered psychotherapy it is necessary to ensure that you have safety nets in place, so you can uncover your deepest and darkest psychological drives without tipping into meltdown. This means you need to establish safe boundaries. There are three ways of doing so.

The first is to choose a therapist and use a course of therapy to confront what you have identified as requiring attention. To put this into a practical context, let's say you have delved into your psyche using the framework we have presented here, and you realise there is a deep blockage on which you can't get a handle. Many people have experienced childhood trauma involving physical or sexual assault. Many also have long-standing issues with parents or siblings, with key underlying emotions and attitudes formed during early childhood subsequently driving and dominating their adult relationships. Others have problems with a particular person, perhaps a boss, a fellow worker, or a competitor, whose presence in their life similarly brings up strong anxieties and emotions. Using a therapist to delve into what is involved is simply a smart use of available resources. Not only does a therapist provide a framework for you to delve into your psyche, the therapist provides a safe, professional environment to help you maintain perspective and balance throughout what is often an unsettling process.

Clearly, there are many kinds of therapists. It is not necessary to find a therapist who is comfortable with the idea that past life experiences may be manifesting in the current life scenario you are investigating. However, it would be helpful to select a therapist who works within a developmental framework rather than a strictly therapeutic one. As we stated in the previous section, much therapy today is geared towards suppressing psychological symptoms through mood-altering drugs, with the limited goal of getting people through the day. The process we are advocating involves what is commonly referred to as talk therapy. This comes in many forms, but we suggest you find a therapist who offers a process for delving into deep psychological drives. Jungian therapists fall into this category, as do many of those who offer psychodynamic therapy.

When consulting a professional therapist, the most effective outcomes are likely to result when you take charge by setting the agenda. That is, you identify the issue you wish to address, and you bring your advance work to the therapy sessions. Of course, the therapist will take charge during the actual sessions, in guiding and aiding you as you delve into your psychic depths. But you remain in charge in the sense that you have undertaken the therapy because you have a specific issue to address. Note we do not say "a specific goal to achieve" because the most effective therapy will take you into places of which you weren't previously consciously aware. Having a rigid cause or outcome in mind before starting therapy will hold you back from opening up subtle aspects that are likely crucial to what has shaped you in the past. So having a focus on an area of your psyche that you are addressing, but leaving the process open as to where you will go in investigating that area, is likely to provide the deepest insights.

We repeat, the advantage in consulting a professional psychotherapist is that they naturally provide perspective and balance as part of their practice.

This doesn't guarantee you won't experience some level of inner meltdown—confronting your past traumas and missteps is never straightforward—but it does provide a safety net to catch you if you tip over.

We note one other way people commonly use professionals. This is to consult a psychic in order to find out about the past, or attend a workshop that is designed to bring psychological blockages to the fore. If the psychic or workshop doesn't provide talk therapy around what is drudged up, then essentially what is happening is that the enquirer is getting new information that they then have to process by themselves. This is a different situation to what we have just described, in which a psychotherapist facilitates the process of you opening up Pandora's Box, but then also helps you process what you uncover. (We will address the topic of using professionals to dig up information outside a therapeutic context shortly.)

Consulting a professional psychotherapist, then, is one approach to safely delve into your psyche. There are two other approaches that may be safely applied. One is in a group context, the second is on your own. We will comment on each in turn. But first we need to clarify what we are doing.

THE PROCESS OF SELF-ENQUIRY

At this point it is useful to identify the process of self-transformation we are advocating as self-enquiry. Self-enquiry is a developmental psychological process in which spiritual seekers address the circumstances of their life by delving into the psychological traits that have brought those circumstances into existence, and that continue to shape how you act in them. Because traits in this life do not stand alone, but exist in relationship to past life experiences and your prior responses to those experiences, self-enquiry is multi-life in its focus. Its purpose is to identify specific traits that aid or stifle individuals as they work through the life situations they have planned this time round.

Self-enquiry is a spiritual practice because, in the widest sense, you have incarnated in a human body, and taken on the yoke of human existence, in order to evolve as a spiritual identity. On the spiritual level, you made a plan for what you wish to achieve in this life. Self-enquiry is designed to help you maximise your life plan by identifying and so enabling you to foster those traits and factors in your life that promote your development, and to identify and diminish the impact of those factors that stifle your development.

This is the way that self-enquiry can be used as a means for self-transformation. It is designed to help you maximise what you achieve of your life plan this time round, and so take you further towards the ultimate goal you are aiming to achieve as an incarnating human being, that of becoming a knowing, loving and wise individual.

As we just observed, there are two major contexts for engaging in self-enquiry. These are in a group context and flying solo. This is what we will consider next.

CHAPTER 14

Group vs Solo Self-Enquiry

W E HAVE PREVIOUSLY DISCUSSED USING GROUPS FOR SELF-enquiry in a book titled *How Did I End Up Here?* There we devoted several chapters to considering practical issues with respect to organising a group. We recommend reading those chapters to get another perspective on the following comments. Here we will largely discuss group self-enquiry in psychological terms, focusing on the relevance of group-based self-enquiry to achieving self-transformation.

The single greatest advantage group self-enquiry offers over solo efforts is that it provides a context for attendees to share their experiences and explain how they have processed their experiences. Individuals each have their own personal band of experience. When working alone, this often narrow band of experiences provides the primary experiential data they have to work with. Group meetings offer the opportunity to pool experiences and so extend the available data. Because people rarely experience the same situations in exactly the same way, and because they process what has happened to them from a variety of perspectives, and because they derive different lessons from their experiences, hearing what others have to say when they were faced with similar situations to your own can provide multiple insights it would otherwise take many lifetimes to accumulate. This is the single greatest advantage group meetings offer any who seek to enquire into the psychological what, how and why of their existence.

For group self-enquiry to work to its maximum benefit, everyone attending has to stand back from their own experiences, put aside self-defensiveness and self-judgement, and treat what they offer up to group scrutiny as contributions to the group's accumulating experiential library of case studies. In effect, attendee's shared experiences provide case studies containing experiential data, from which each may extract relevant lessons and apply them to their own self-transformation.

At this point, it will be useful to direct this discussion of group meetings into a brief consideration the role of teachers and gurus.

TUTORS, TEACHERS, GURUS

In spiritual circles over the last several thousand years it has become customary for groups to be lead by a teacher. This means groups become constituted of a single leader and multiple student followers. In practice, a leader often appoints a small number of experienced students to the position of lieutenant. However, this doesn't change the basic status of people within the group: there is a single leader, and there are multiple followers.

It is certainly understandable that in many situations an individual may possess superior expertise, and that others may learn from that person. In the trades this results in there being a master and apprentices; in education, a professor and students. That this same hierarchy operates in psychospiritual study groups is natural. Nonetheless, there are difficulties inherent in the spiritual teacher-student relationship. To delve into this topic, we will divide those who help others in their spiritual endeavours into the three broad categories of tutor, teacher and guru.

The title *tutor* may be applied in its broadest sense to any person who has expertise in a specific human activity, and uses a learning environment to share what they know. Such sharing often occurs in work situations, such as when a master builder or chef teaches apprentices skills while they are all working on a job. An alternative learning environment is provided by short workshops, which people attend to learn specific skills. In the context of psychospiritual development, people most commonly sign up to workshops for varying periods: a few hours, a weekend, several days, even several months. Those attending workshops do so to learn from the tutors' experience-based outlook and to enhance their own skills by absorbing what the tutors have discovered worked for them over the years. The focus of these types of workshops tends to be practical and skills-focused. It's a short burt of knowledge exchange: when the workshop is over, tutor and attendees go their separate ways.

The relationship between teacher and student is more complex. The complexity develops when students attend meetings over an extended period. Repeated contacts between student and teacher naturally provide an opportunity for them to get to know one another personally. How well, and how intricate their interactions become, depends on opportunity and intent. It is well documented in spiritual circles that the teacher-student relationship may become inappropriately sexual, or develop into a relationship involving dominance/subservience and bullying. This is a potential downside of extended teacher-student relations. The upside, which results when teacher and pupil each adopt a detached attitude when examining the student's deep issues, is that the teacher is able to observe students over an extended period, and students get the chance to share what troubles them. As a result, the opportunity exists to open the Pandora's Box of the student's psyche and get to the bottom of troubling psychological traits and behaviours. This work is reinforced by the student reporting back to the group what is found and worked through.

What we are identifying as *guru* is an extension of the teacher-student relationship. The guru scenario arises when students see the teacher as being on an extremely elevated spiritual level compared to them. Students may go so far as to accord the guru god-like status. Then the student, in effect, is no longer a student but becomes a worshipper. In Eastern spiritual traditions the notion of the all-knowing guru is widespread. This same notion of the guru was imported into the West during the 1970s, and subsequently became prevalent in spiritual circles. Of course, Western Christianity already had its own model of the guru, manifest in the supposition that the priest is closer to God than ordinary worshippers, with the result that their advice and blessings were considered to come from a higher source. In this scenario, followers worship God through the guru-priest.

To make our position clear on tutors, teachers and gurus, we view the short-term tutor-attendee relationship to be very spiritually useful for all concerned. Similarly, the teacher-student is very useful, but with the caveat that both positive and negative psychological links will develop during a long-term relationship. However, we don't see there being any benefit when students give the teacher god-like guru status. In order to clarify this view, we need to comment further on the teacher-student relationship.

TEACHERS, STUDENTS AND LIFE PLANS

When anyone chooses to attend a spiritual group long-term, in the vast majority of instances it is because it is part of their life plan. So if you are now, or have previously attended a spiritual group's meetings for an extended period, it is because before you incarnated you decided attending a spiritually oriented group would be beneficial to your development. This is a choice numerous people make. The flip side of this is that the teacher also selected a life plan that incorporated becoming a spiritual teacher, similarly to enhance their own development. So underpinning the teacher-pupil relationship is the intent on each person's part to use this situation as an opportunity to develop.

What this means is that neither teacher nor students are the finished product. All are engaged in group meetings because the situation offers them opportunities to develop. This must not be forgotten. Certainly, the teacher is likely to possess more expertise in certain aspects of psychospiritual development. (Although, as we have noted elsewhere, this is not necessarily be the case, for the student may be younger or know less than the teacher, but actually have lived many more lives, and so have a base skill level within their accumulated human identity that far outstrips the teacher's.) This means that the group exists for mutually beneficial purposes.

Teachers have all kinds of experiences to draw on and expertise they have developed over the years. Many have the ability to create an environment students find beneficial on varying levels, and this draws them back to group meetings year after year. However, students' negative psychological traits may equally draw them back.

One of the most prevalent negative traits that hold students and teachers together is dependence. Dependence may be one-sided, with the student projecting onto the teacher an idealised mother or father figure, or it may be mutual, with the teacher relishing the admiration students cast their way and the status being a teacher gives them. The intensity of the dependence increases manyfold when the student treats the teacher as a guru and starts revering them as having god-like powers.

The biggest problem with dependence for students is they end up surrendering their volition and judgement to another person. It could be argued that just as a child knows too little to have their own volition and judgement, and so needs to be guided by a parent who effectively runs their life for them, so the student starting out on a path of psychospiritual development knows very little and therefore needs the teacher/guru to guide them in their decision-making. We would make several comments in response.

First, the process of self-enquiry, as we are describing it here, is for people who have entered at least the teen part of their development, which is equivalent to the initial feline portion of their reincarnational trajectory. This means they—and you, our reader—are not naive beginners. You have considerable multi-life experience, and so have many resources to draw on that already exist within your accumulated human identity.

Second, no teacher is all-knowing. In term of skills, teachers have some skills that are developed to a high level, and others they are still developing. This means they also have weaknesses. So not everything the teacher decrees has equal validity. The student needs to be aware of this.

Third, the group situation is itself an experiential environment that offers opportunities to learn and grow. Interactions with others in the group, including both the teacher and other students, result in emotional and intellectual synergies and psychological frictions. Individuals may have pre-planned, prior to incarnating, to meet within the group in order to resolve karma or to support each other as they work on developing chosen skills. Equally, they may have planned to meet, and to rub each other the wrong way, in order to work through emotions and attitudes they have selected from their deep essence.

Fourth, the teacher is also using the group situation to work through his or her own issues. It takes repeated effort to develop detachment, to overcome judgement, and to learn when to step in to help another who is struggling and when to let them work it out for themselves. Because, like students, they are learning, teachers make mistakes. It is an inevitable aspect of the process of developing in the human domain.

All this equally applies to the worshipper-guru scenario, with the added problem that the student puts the teacher up on a pedestal, which means they give themselves a correspondingly lowly spiritual status. There are many reasons people do this.

PUTTING A TEACHER ON A PEDESTAL

On one level, putting the teacher on a pedestal can be useful to people whose life plan is mostly outwardly directed, in the sense that it involves much action and little introspection. Acknowledging an individual as being "up there", and worshipping them from afar, as people do with the Pope and the Dalai Lama, functions as a reminder that a spiritual dimension exists, and that it will be returned to in due course.

In this type of reverence, acknowledgement of a deeper reality is often subconscious. Nonetheless, the reverence performs the important function of providing a spiritual reminder that acts as a minor balance in their otherwise outwardly-focused life this time round. For such people, the culmination of their worship involves getting the darshan of their guru, that is, being in their physical presence. Once they gain this, their spiritual yearnings are satisfied. We note that sacred temples, shrines and sites perform the same function for many people, serving to help them feel connected to a supposed "higher" spiritual reality.

This is all useful, because only a small percentage of incarnated individuals choose to incorporate intense psychospiritual development in their life plan during any era. But for those who have chosen to do so, and who are currently attending a spiritual group of any kind, we repeat, such a reverential attitude is not conducive to inner development.

We wish to make one final point regarding the guru-worshipper relationship. This is that many enter it passively. This is, they expect the guru to tell them how their life is. In effect, this means they stop thinking for themselves. In ordinary learning, people need to opportunity to try things out for themselves, learn what works experientially, and decide what they will continue with and what they won't. This is how children absorb so much during the brief years of childhood. Therefore to surrender the process of learning to be spiritual to another person, allowing them to dictate what you should or should not do in your life, especially when the guru is so distant you will likely never interact with them, makes no developmental sense.

For this reason we return to the concept of self-enquiry.

QUESTIONING GROUP MEMBERSHIP

Those who wish to investigate their spiritual depths, and are using a group situation to do so, are advised to enquire into their own reasons for joining the group, how they relate to the teacher, and what keeps them returning week after week. Often, it will be found that positive and negative traits are intertwined. So an individual may have pre-planned to join a group led by a particular individual as teacher—a person with whom they may or may not have had previous life interactions—and while the aim is to enhance certain skills and abilities, those skills and abilities may come with certain negative traits embedded in them. Accordingly, it pays to enquire into whether your psyche contains traits such as dependence, a sense of inferiority, lack of self-esteem, arrogance, pride, a sense of superiority (many like to imagine their teacher and group are superior to all other teachers and groups), or too much self-satisfaction, to the degree that you feel you have "arrived" and don't need to work any more on your development. The exercise of appraising your experience of being in a group offers the opportunity to face up and work on traits that impede your development in a group context.

We have spent some time on this topic because it is rarely sufficiently appreciated. People usually enter a spiritual group with high hopes, then, perhaps years later, just end up feeling they have been spat out the other side. Having balance in your expectations, and appreciating that there are pluses and minuses in every human endeavour, will prevent the build up of unrealistic expectations, misunderstandings, and resentments when things don't turn out as expected.

The bottom line in our advice here is that groups provide opportunities for learning. Expecting a group, or another individual, to provide you with *all* the answers you feel you need to develop, isn't realistic. Ultimately, such an expectation isn't in your own best developmental interests.

WORKING SOLO

We conclude by considering the advantages and limitations of solo self-enquiry versus practising in a group context.

Certainly, not everyone is comfortable talking and sharing in a group context, especially when the group is large. Additionally, some people are naturally gregarious, so easily dominate group discussions. Others are comparatively wilting violets, and can only bring themselves to discuss what troubles them when talking to the teacher face to face. But they need to be part of the group in order to get the opportunity to talk to the teacher one-on-one. In the meantime, they learn much from other group attendees' experiences. And the group environment itself stimulates them to enquire more deeply into their psychospiritual make-up. This is all part of the trade-offs of being in a group.

When committing to a solo course of self-enquiry, the big issue is maintaining momentum. That, in turn, itself requires constant stimulation. We observe it is certainly difficult to sustain self-enquiry on one's own. In a group, one of the teacher's tasks is to keep prodding people, pushing them into seeing themselves anew, and prompting them to face up to aspects of their psyche that their false personality would otherwise keep in the basement. So the tricky task for the solo self-enquirer is to keep prodding themselves. There are a number of ways to achieve this.

The most widely practised way is to keep a journal. Regular entries, whether weekly, daily, or just when something strikes you, is helpful. Indeed, those who are attending group meetings will find it worthwhile keeping a journal for their own records. It is useful having written entries you can look back on and be reminded of what you did, felt and thought at a previous time. It will also highlight issues that repeatedly come up, that need to be addressed.

For the individual engaged in solo self-enquiry, the challenge is to find new stimulus, new inputs, that challenge their thinking and prompt them to see themselves in new ways. reading relevant books is useful, of course. So is attending talks and short workshops, specifically to seek new information and pick up new skills. But behind all inner works what is needed is constant self-questioning. We don't mean this in the sense of undermining yourself by questioning what you have achieved. We mean in the developmental sense we vare discussing here: of seeking to learn ever about the who, what and why of your existence. And to achieve not generalised knowledge about such things, but to learn about the who, what and why of what makes you tick.

Meditation can be a useful means for contacting your spiritual self and accessing what it knows. Information is released on a need-to-know basis. This means it is only by posing a question regarding an aspect of your psyche or life that an answer will arrive: no question, no answer. We have discussed in some detail the process of using meditation to access deep information in *Where Do I Go When I Meditate?*

Dreams offer another way to access deep information. Before going to sleep, pose a question, holding it in your mind. Then, when you wake, write down whatever is present in your mind. It may be a symbolic dream, a feeling, or a thought. It takes practice before dreams (or meditation) provide answers to your questions, but they can be very effective, given you are posing the question to your own multi-layered spiritual self, which knows far more than you do, given you operate within the confines of your embodied mind. If your spiritual self doesn't know the answer, it can seek the answer from another, more experienced source. And each answer naturally opens up new lines of enquiry.

ON SEEKING INFORMATION FROM OTHERS

We return at this point to the issue of consulting psychics when seeking answers regarding the who, what and why of your existence. It may seem consulting a medium offers an easy alternative to using meditating or dreaming. However, doing so is not straightforward. All psychics have their own skills, and their own experiential base. They also have their own strengths and blind spots. So finding a psychic who is in tune with the information you require does not merely involve finding someone and paying them. You may have to meditate or ask for a dream to find one who is suitable!

Several factors enter into the psychic-seeker scenario. Two are very relevant to this discussion. First, genuine psychics generally access a limited number of non-embodied sources. The psychic-source relationship is built on these sources having a particular focus or skill. For example, the psychic may be a medium who answers questions regarding deceased family and friends. The source may be very skilled at accessing the deceased and obtaining information from them to convey back to the medium, who in turn passes it on to the grieving enquirer. Or the medium may perceive the deceased directly. But this same medium-source relationship may not be skilful at accessing past life information. For that another psychic skilled at obtaining that information is required.

The chain via which information is passed leads to another difficulty with consulting psychics. This is that the information passes through the psychic to the enquirer. And every embodied human mind is, in effect, a filtering device. Each mind has its own strengths and weaknesses. So the psychic may receive information from a non-embodied source, but express it in words that are coloured by the psychic's own preferences or even biases. The psychic may not pick up on a subtle aspect of the information - because the information is received non-verbally, so needs to be translated into words before it can be passed on, and speech being a coarser medium than thought, much subtly can be lost in the translation from one to the other. Finally, the psychic may not be aware of the significance of a small, apparently minor point, that actually is the nub of what the enquirer is seeking. So while consulting a medium may be illuminating, or equally may not. Or the exchange may only provide part of what the enquirer seeks.

Of course, the same process applies when you use meditation or dreams to seek information. Your own preferences or biases may colour the information you receive. You may end up focusing on a secondary aspect, and not actually receive the most significant part of the information, due to your expectations, or because are are so focused on what seems to you to be primary, that you ignore another aspect that, in the long-term, may turn out actually to be primary. This is why we suggest you write down what you receive immediately after receiving it. Relying on memory is uncertain: your mind is unreliable, it forgets,and in time certain aspects of any experience tend to be remembered most intensely while other aspects fall away. In addition, sometimes you just need time to process all the implications of information.

Everyone has had the experience of remembering something from the past, and perhaps years later talking to another who participated in the same event, whose perspective is entirely different and suddenly see what occurred in an entirely new light. That is what can happen with information: as you gain greater experience, and so develop new perspectives, information received long ago may be seen differently and stimulate entirely new insights. Remaining open to such developments, and pushing yourself to keep seeking them, is fundamental to successfully engaging in solo self-enquiry.

Having commented on the broad psychological parameters of group and solo self-enquiry, we now pass on to the central topic of this series of books: using self-enquiry to develop your psychospiritual insight and becoming a fuller, deeper, more rounded human being.

CHAPTER 15

Using Self-Enquiry
For Self-Transformation

THE KEY RATIONALE FOR ENGAGING IN THE PROCESS OF SELF-enquiry is not limited to understanding the who, what and why of your psyche. The purpose is to change it. We conclude this book by summing up the transformational process. To do so we will reiterate a number of points.

Where the practice of self-enquiry begins is with the realisation that the circumstances of your life, including the key factors that have structured your life circumstances and the key psychological traits that have driven your responses to these structural factors, are part of your life plan. They have been chosen by you. You have chosen them because they are what you, at the level of your spiritual self, have decided to work with in this life.

You, our reader, may respond to this statement by observing that we have already made this plain. But it needs to be repeated because it is fundamental to appreciating what it going on in your life. It means that if you are faced with shit, it is your shit. If you experience joy, it is your joy. Whatever challenges and satisfactions you face, they are your challenges and satisfactions. They have been specificially designed by you, for you.

This must be taken on board in order to appreciate why the process of self-enquiry is *spiritually* significant. All the key situations of your current life have been chosen by you to aid your ongoing evolution. All the psychological traits present in your psyche, positive and negative, nurturing and self-limiting, which come to the fore in response to life situations, are drawn from the deep essence stores of your accumulated human identity. It means these traits are in your incarnated essence self now because you created them during prior incarnations and you wish to work on and with them now.

So when you enquire into the nitty-gritty of your current life, what you are also doing, at a deep level, is investigating your own incarnational self. You are delving into the multi-life reality of who you really are. This is what is at the heart of self-enquiry. It leads you from your socialised self, into your essence self, and beyond it into your spiritual self. And when you make a consciousness connection with your spiritual self, you start to integrate aspects of your non-embodied spiritual self with the human sub-personality who is "you" this time round.

But to achieve all this, you need to change how you currently function. This is the point of engaging in any form of spiritual practice, including self-enquiry.

WHAT SUCCESSFUL SELF-ENQUIRERS NEED

The practice of self-enquiry that we are advocating here may, in therapeutic terms, be called a form of talk therapy. Whether you carry out your practice in a group, and discuss your psychospiritual work with others, or practise solo, talking to yourself via your journal, what you are doing is bringing into your everyday mind aspects of your psyche that are hidden and so are unconscious, and usually function automatically.

The purpose of providing the concepts in the foregoing pages is to give you tools to help you identify your own psychological behaviour and traits that otherwise would remain buried and unacknowledged. The tools on offer are conceptual tools, designed to help you analyse your feelings, thoughts and behaviour, bringing the hidden factors that have shaped them out of the basement and exposing them in the light of day.

We have previously commented that doing this requires courage. Bringing stuff up out of the basement isn't an easy task, especially when much of it involves pain and trauma, and the worst of your own reactive feelings and behaviour. As we also noted earlier, the way to successfully achieve this is by stepping back inside yourself. By taking an analytical position, by looking at the stuff from the basement at arms length, you take the emotional sting out of them. You make examining them palatable—as much as such a process might be called palatable. We note two approaches help you step back.

One is to use your intellect to examine your emotions. You can't reflect on psychological traits when you are still floundering in the emotions involved. You can only reflect when you are in a calm inner state. Shifting your awareness into your intellect, separating from your churning emotions, enables you to do this. Ultimately, the skill you need to develop is the ability to see yourself as others do, without attachment and self-defensiveness.

Our recommended second approach aids the required detachment. It is to see yourself as a multi-incarnational being. You, at the spiritual level, are a being who includes multiple human sub-personalities within its accumulated identity. You, the person who is reading these pages, is no less, and certainly no more, than a sub-identity of your ongoing spiritual self. All your spiritual self's sub-identities have their own experiences, their own charactistics, their own successes and failures. None is more right or wrong than any other. Collectively, they constitute the being who is you on the spiritual level. If you can step back from yourself and adopt this wider view, it will again help take the sting out of your limitations and errors. You transcend them all.

We realise this second approach is a somewhat abstract prescription for dealing with the turmoils of being human. Nonetheless, adopting a multi-life perspective has the potential to take the pressure off and allow you more freedom to act. And, as a corollary, more freedom to enjoy the person you are this time round.

There will only ever be one "you", even for you. So make the most of the opportunity. If there is narrowness of occupation and interests, go into them with energy. If there is uncertainty, explore that uncertainty. If you have a talent that you are struggling to find space for in your life, work on that. Investigate it. Nurture it. Wrestle with the situation. Examine the limiting factors. It is all part of being human. The worst thing you can do is not do anything at all. Unless, of course, that is your life plan. How will you know? By looking hard at yourself, analysing what is going on, identifying key psychological traits, figuring out how they function, how they interact with each other, and how they arose in the first place.

That is what it is to be human.

THE SELF-ENQUIRERS' SKILL

To conclude, we observe that success in understanding who you are involves sustaining two apparently opposed activities simultaneously.

The first, as we just commented, is to fully engage with the circumstances of your life. Don't hold back out of fear of screwing up. No set of human behaviours is full and rounded. It is likely that what you do in pursuing your life goals will, from time to time, upset others around you, even those you love. Pursuing your goals will also, at times, upset, confuse and befuddle you. That is the deal. The important thing is that you engage with your life's possibilities to the fullest extent you are able. That you take advantage of what you yourself have planned.

On the other hand, it is useful to nurture a part of your self that, when you wish, can extract itself from your life's ongoing goal-chasing, so you may stand aside and impartially examine what you are feeling, thinking and doing. Such an ability is fostered through the practice of self-enquiry. That is why we recommend it.

In stating this, we consider it is not sufficient to just detach yourself from your life, such as people do during prayer and meditation. By incarnating, you are literally putting your life on the line. The best spiritual practices acknowledge this and don't just help you disconnect from the world around you, or the desires you experience towards it. More helpfully, they take you deeper inside your self. And they bring you face to face with what, in some circles, is called the dweller on the threshold—all those negative psychological factors, that we have labelled false personality, that prevent you from entering your deep self and learning who you are. Ultimately, spirituality is not about feeling good about yourself and feeling at one with the universe—although we do acknowledge such experiences are important aids to understanding the wider context of your existence in the kosmos. Rather, we are emphasising the degree to which obtaining a spiritual perspective is difficult and requires sustained effort, starting with the effort to overcome your own limitations. To perceive the kosmos from a different perspective, you need to change where you're looking from. And that requires you to change yourself, because you are perceiving through the lens of your own being.

With that, we end this sequence of three books, incorporating *Experimental Spirituality*, *Practical Spirituality* and *Psychological Spirituality*. They have been designed to provide a template for psychospiritual development suited to those living in the twenty-first century. We have expressly removed religious connections, and emphasised the psychological, in an attempt to provide clarity. We almost added "simplicity" to "clarity", then decided not. This is because while we consider from our perspective that these three books offer a very simplified view of what is involved in human incarnation, we are conscious that anyone first coming across them will find material that is increasingly complex and detailed, culminating in this book, which we have tried to keep straightforward, but is still a dense read.

Our intention in writing these books is that they will be used as workbooks for those who wish to undertake a course in self-enquiry. We have tried to structure the material so it progressively builds into a rich template for self-discovery. In doing so, we have purloined material from a range of sources. We say "purloined" with our tongue metaphorically in our cheek because, of course, no one owns any of this material. It is humanity's, largely given to it by those who have completed their own time on Earth, using what they have learned to generate texts that they know, from personal experience, will be of benefit to those who seek to lift the veil and peek into what lies beyond everyday perception.

There will be a gap in time before the final two books in this series are completed, due to various factors needing to fall into place, and other books needing to be written. In the meantime, we hope all who seek to know more about themselves will find their endeavours are fruitful. We particularly acknowledge those who have had the tenacity to work their way through to this page. We are very aware that there is a great deal of information to absorb. We wish you well in your efforts to process it. Above all, just as we have initiated this series to share useful information with those who need it, so we hope you, our reader, will pass on to others whatever material you have found personally useful, whether in part or in whole, and in accordance with the contexts you find yourself.

Until next time, *au revoir*.

Glossary

Accumulated human identity   The sum total of what an identity has experienced, felt, thought and done during the course of each human incarnation. At the end of each life these are uploaded to the ongoing spiritual self. The experiences of the biological, socialised and essence selves are stored as deep essence traits. They are part of an even larger store of experiential material, which includes: experiences resulting from choices made, neglected or rejected; repeated behaviours, changed behaviours, repeated reactions to others' behaviours; successes, mistakes and lessons learned; and skills, abilities and talents developed in the many fields of human activity. There is a store of karma, a store of obligations (which results from as yet unfulfilled promises made to reciprocate help received), and a store of goodwill, which incorporates the largess of compassion, benevolence, love.

Attachment   Attachment is a by-product of identification. When a spiritual identity identifies with its body as being its self it also naturally becomes attached to the people, objects, places, situations and experiences that form the texture of its daily activities and interactions. These attachments are physical, social and psychological in nature.

Attitude   Attitude works with life goal and orientation. Situated in the essence self, it steers the individual towards situations required to fulfil the life plan and away from those that don't. There are seven attitudes, which fall into three pairs: realist and cynic, spiritualist and stoic, idealist and sceptic, and self-pragmatist. One attitude is chosen for the course of a life in order to help fulfil the life plan.

Biological self   The body. Its physical characteristics are shaped by genetic inheritance. It contains and sustains the human sensory and nervous systems, along with the brain and its cognitive functions that process perceptions and so underpin every-day awareness. One of the struggles an incarnating spirit has with the biological self is coping with its instinctive urges, personally and at the social level. Socialisation has transformed all instinctive urges: the urge to procreate has been socialised into marriage and mortgages, the urge to eat into working for money to buy food, etc.

Bliss   The biological self experiences pleasure. The essence self experiences the happiness of fulfilling long-term activities. Bliss arises from the expression of the spiritual self. Insofar as the spirit is able to express itself to its satisfaction during the course of its life, it achieves bliss.

Chief feature   The crystallisation of a core fear within the socialised self. Various psychological coping and defense mechanisms form around the core fear, creating the edifice of chief fea-ture. Chief feature, with its underlying fear, its inwardly focused self-calming and various psychological coping mechanisms, along with its outwardly-directed behaviours, collectively provide the foundations for the false personality.

Conditioned reactions   Automatically performed reactions to life situations. They include responses, attitudes and ideas about the world inculcated into an individual during childhood, which con-tinue into adulthood. Part of the socialised self, when nega-tive in nature they limit the essence's self's expression so need to be recognised and replaced.

Core disposition   There are seven core dispositions of spiritual identity. The Michael Teachings divide them into the metaphors of serv-ant, artisan, warrior, scholar, sage, priest and king. Core dis-position is further shaped by modality and secondary dis-position to create a unique identity, which also predispose each individual towards a specific kind of bliss.

Crystallisation By adulthood the socialised self has crystallised into rigid identity. What is crystallised are the psychological traits, conditioned reactions and behavioral coping strategies that it embraced in response to the impacts of family, community and culture while growing up. For most, the crystallised socialised self provides their identity for the rest of their lives. The socialised self dissolves when the body dies, so everyone breaks free of it at death. Breaking free before death is more problematic. The outright shattering of crystallised identity would be traumatic, even lethal. Accordingly, rather than shattering the crystallised self, the psychospiritual approach is to chip away at the crystallisation, bit by bit, piece by piece. The practice of self-enquiry offers a process for doing so.

Defensive behaviours When individuals are upset they strive to calm themselves by re-establishing their previous inner equilibrium. In unconsciously acting human beings, this is achieved via the defensive behaviours of denying, justifying, deflecting and attacking. Initially formed during childhood, these four defensive behaviours manifest in all kinds of situations, at all levels of human interaction.

Development When individuals are born their three essence self's centres do not automatically function to their full potential. They need to be developed. The developmental scale is broadly characterised as being from infant, to child, teen and adult. The centres develop as a result of an individual consciously working with them. To reach their full potential, the centres need to be purified of negative emotions, attitudes and behaviours. [Also see *Trajectories*]

Deep essence During the course of each incarnation a spiritual identity experiences human life via a sub-identity, a.k.a. sub-personality. When that sub-identity dies all the experiential data generated during the course of its life is uploaded to the ongoing spiritual identity. Deep essence is the accumulation of all the positive and negative essence level moving, emotional and intellectual qualities and traits that the spiritual identity has experienced, manifested and explored through its many sub-identities. Accordingly, deep essence refers to human qualities, not spiritual qualities.

Emotional centre   With the moving and intellectual centres, one of the three main components of the essence self. Emotions may be positive or negative. Positive emotions include love, compassion, gratitude and the ecstatic emotional states that mystics experience. Negative emotions include self-pity, anxiety, melancholy and despair. The moving part of the emotional centre enables individuals to appreciate the colours, textures and artistry of the world, and make their own contribution to them. The emotional part of the emotional centre is where emotions are experienced. This includes enabling one to enter into the feelings of others. The intellectual aspect of the emotional brain manifests as intuition, which facilitates the making of connections and usually occurs as spontaneous flashes of insight. No centre naturally functions to its highest potential. Negative emotions need to be addressed and overcome in order for the emotional centre to reach adult functioning.

Energetic self   This is an energetic complex that functions on several levels. It includes the energetic envelope that surrounds the body, known as the aura. It also includes energy centres, commonly called chakras, and energies associated with each of the moving, emotional and intellectual centres.

Essence self   The higher level functions of the human animal, characterised here as consisting of the three moving, emotional and intellectual centres. The essence self is where the growth of human abilities and identity occurs.

Everyday awareness   In ordinary terms, the level of awareness manifested by the alert human brain. In the terms designated here, everyday awareness is a function of the active parts of the biological, socialised and essence selves. Shaped by evolutionary needs, the everyday awareness automatically focuses on the world around it to ensure its body's survival. However, it is malleable, and capable of absorbing subtle inputs from the essence self, and beyond that from the energetic and spiritual levels. One of the ultimate aims of embodiment is to imbue the everyday awareness with the intent and awareness of the individual's own spiritual self.

Everyday identity   The identity each individual maintains during daily life. Due to psychological momentum, the drives underlying everyday identity change only marginally as an individual grows from infant to child to teen to adult. However, this situation changes if individuals work on themselves to transform their inner functioning. General maturity can also change inner functioning to a limited degree, such as an uncertain person becoming more confident due to social endorsement. Yet while some aspects of everyday identity are projected onto an individual by others, most are constructed by individuals in response to growing up. Psychological impositions and trauma significantly influence the nature of everyday identity, which only changes through deliberate work to transform it.

Evolution   Personal spiritual evolution is a process in which identities undertake an extended series of incarnations to develop their innate core spiritual disposition. The goal is to deliberately sow, harvest and process human experiences in order to gain mastery of self-selected situations, processes and skill sets. The process of gaining mastery generates experiential data that helps the essence self grow during each incarnation. Uploaded to the accumulated human identity at death, this data contributes to the evolution of the individual's spiritual self.

False personality   More properly called the obstacle personality, this is the collection of largely negative and defensive feelings, thoughts and behaviours that are centred around chief feature. When negative and defensive feelings, thoughts and behaviours dominate the everyday awareness, usually in response to external pressures, false personality's negativities can leak into the essence self and send it into its negative poles. Psychologically, it presents inner obstacles that need to be overcome for the individual to fully express itself via its essence self and fulfil its life plan.

Fear   Suppressed fear lies at the heart of chief feature and therefore of false personality. There are two fundamental sources of fear. The first is the existential fear a naive spiritual identity feels on first being embodied in the human domain and finds it is unable to control the body in which it dwells. The second is the fear emanating from the old brain, an animal defense mechanism that manifests as flight or flight. This animal fear has been socialised over the eons and now manifests in subtle behaviours. As a result fear has become embedded in human culture. A variety of different socialised fears drive the psychological make-up of everyday identity. The Michael Teachings identity these seven fears as the fear of not having enough, of being vulnerable, of missing out, of being inadequate, of being worthless, of losing control, and of the new. Each socialised identity is driven by one of these fears, which is usually selected prior to incarnation, then reinforced during childhood experiences. Self-calming and defensive behaviours are used to cover up fear, which then becomes deeply buried within the socialised self. Fear fuels the many psychological factors that limit an individual's ability to make the most of opportunities.

Five-layered self   A model that proposes the human self consists of five layers: the biological self, the socialised self, the essence self, the energetic self, the spiritual self.

Forgetfulness   Forgetfulness is an advantage for spiritual identities when they incarnate because it enables them to forget what they experienced during previous incarnations, forget even that they *are* an embodied spiritual identity. This enables them to experience their current life in a fresh and open way. Forgetfulness is a disadvantage because it stops individuals from remembering why they are here, living the life they are, with the people they are.

Growth   Human growth requires the right conditions. The body needs nutrition, while the socialised self needs language, education, nurturing. Developmental growth occurs at the level of the essence self. In order to develop, the essence self needs to express itself and requires repeated opportunities to practice its abilities. If these are deficient, individuals will not reach their essence growth potential in this life.

Identification   A state in which an individual's everyday awareness and sense of personal identity is limited to the experience of being a body. The spiritual dimension of identity is forgotten. Identification is important for reinforcing forgetfulness. The negative result is when the individual identifies with false personality. The practice of stepping back within is important for working against the impact of identification.

Identity   Identity exists on many levels. External identity consists of bodily and socially constructed identity. Internal identity consists of the self-image one constructs for oneself. Essence level identity reflects practical, emotional and intellectual abilities and expertise. Everyday identity is the identity people project and protect during daily interactions. Underlying them all is spiritual identity, the ongoing identity that uses external, internal, essence and everyday identity to live a human existence.

Inner cues   Inner cues come from the spiritual self. They consist of impulses that manifest in the everyday awareness as feelings, thoughts or an inexplicable urge to make a certain choice or to follow a particular line of activity. In general, inner cues help people fulfil their life plan.

Inner-outer synergy   Simply, everyday awareness responds to outward stimuli according to its psychological make-up. More specifically, an individual's awareness latches onto certain things in the external world because they resonate with the person's inner impulses and traits. Thus a person's traits and predilections lead them to reach out to and latch onto particular people, objects and events. At the same time, ignore other people, objects and events are ignore because they don't inwardly resonate. Thus the attachments and identifications that keep anyone engaged with select aspects of everyday life are the result of inner-outer synergy. This equally applies to essence traits, which similarly latch onto and ignore opportunities according to whether or not they resonate with the life plan. All this occurs without the everyday mind's conscious choice.

Intellectual centre   With the moving and emotional centres, one of the three main components of the essence self. The moving part of the intellectual brain, called the formatory apparatus, is an organiser. It organises, categorises and compares concepts. The emotional part of the intellectual centre manifests in the way human beings respond to the sight of stars in the night sky with awe, wonder at powerful and beautiful landscapes, and humility when contemplating the vastness of the stars in the night sky. The intellect of the intellectual centre manifests in abstract thinking. It identifies patterns of many kinds, whether sub-atomic, biological, philosophic, artistic, theological, mechanical, electrical or cosmological in nature.

Intention   Intention ultimately emanates from the spiritual self. All spiritual identities intend to use the experiences gained during their incarnation in a human body to learn, to transform their functioning at all levels of their layered self, and evolve as a spiritual being. The life plan is the extension of a spiritual identity's intention into the essence self level within the human realm. Forgetfulness, identification, attachments, negativities and self-imposed limitations blunt intention.

Karma
Karma = motivation + action + consequence. These form a unit of karma. Karma results when one person impinges on another. There are three grades of impinging: minor, intermediate and major. Minor impinging requires a change of motivation and inner attitude. Major impinging requires the individuals concerned to meet in an incarnated state and resolve their issues. The resolution of intermediate impinging depends on circumstances. Dissolving negative motivations is crucial to resolving all levels of karma.

Kosmos
From the Greek, *kosmos*, meaning order or world. It is used to encompass all that is, accessible and hidden, material and immaterial, physical and spiritual. What we call the physical cosmos, a.k.a. the universe, is part of the kosmos, as are intangible perceptual modalities, along with what we notionally identify as spiritual. In the book titled *The Kosmic Web*, the kosmos is described as incorporating the electrophysical, electromagnetic and electrospiritual modalities of reality.

Life goal
The life goal is a psychological trait that functions at the essence level. It is a concept developed within the Michael Teachings, which identifies seven life goals: growth, revaluation, dominance, submission, acceptance, rejection and maintaining equilibrium.

Life lessons
Whenever individuals go through an experience, review it, and come to understand what they did correctly and what incorrectly, that experience becomes a life lesson. Life lessons come in many forms, may be short or long in duration, and occur in every kind of situation. They lead to mastery in any of the many fields of human endeavour. Reviewing experiences can happen while living a life, but most people extract life lessons after a life has been lived.

Life plan
A plan shaped by a spiritual identity prior to its incarnation.

The life plan provides the basis for the experiment that is an individual life. Incarnated individuals have the choice of keeping to a life plan, abandoning it, or applying it partially. Part of the experiment that is incarnation is to see how the identity copes with what it has organised for itself to experience and learn during that life. Lives that abandon a life plan are not failed experiments. They are merely alternative experiments, and have equal value, because all experiences provide life lessons and so may feed an individual's evolution. Abandoned life plans are usually taken up again in subsequent incarnations in an adjusted form.

Maturity   The purpose of incarnation is for spiritual identities to use the opportunity to mature. Maturing involves building skills and talents to a level of mastery and learning to navigate successfully through any and all human situations. Achieving this requires individuals to extract life lessons from experiences. The process of maturing is reflected in development at the essence self level. A mature human being is acknowledged as being loving, knowledgeable and wise and results the individual no longer needing to incarnate.

Meditation   A state of inner or dual awareness which is achieved by practising one of many techniques that promote internal or external focus. The body may be kept still or in rhythmic movement for the duration of the state. Meditation is differentiated from sleep by continuous mental alertness. An essential function is it offers a way to establish a bridge between spiritual identity and everyday human identity.

Modality   Modulates the expression of a spiritual identity's core disposition. There are three modalities: inward, outward and expressive. A spirit dominated by the inward modality naturally has a contemplative response to life experiences. A spirit dominated by the outward modality naturally tends towards giving themselves over to participating in life experiences, initiating actions. A spirit dominated by the expressive modality naturally seeks to give outward expression to inward thoughts and feelings. In practice, different percentages of each modality is present in individuals, contributing to their unique deep make-up.

Momentum   Each individual has two primary momentums in this life, one emanating from the everyday self and the second from the essence self. The everyday self's momentum results from the psychological mass generated by the five factors of culture, roles, routines, habitual behaviours and conditioned reactions. The positive result of this momentum is that it gives individuals the feeling that they are the same person from one day to the next. The negative result is that everyday momentum keeps an individual travelling along the same inner lanes for years on end, repeating the same thoughts, having the same feelings, and doing the same things. Alternative to the momentum of everyday identity is the momentum of the essence self and its life plan. Inner development requires individuals to jump momentums, from the everyday self to the essence self.

Moving centre   One of the three principal components of the essence self. The emotional part of the moving centre manifests in body-focused emotions, the two most common forms of which are instinctive and adrenal. Positive moving emotions include the physical joy derived from marching, dancing, playing sport or gardening. Instinctive emotions include those involved in mating and nurturing children. Adrenaline emotions are used in sport and physical confrontation. When the instinctive and adrenaline emotions reinforce each other, as they do in territorial and ownership disputes, they can become destructive. The intellect of the moving centre provides common sense, used to think through practical issues and problems.

Multi-life perspective   The proposition that each life be seen as just one in a sequence of related lives. Advantages and disadvantages in this life, pressures and opportunities, urges and inhibitions, are nor randomly present in a life, but have been chosen on the basis of past life choices, and will generate future opportunities. As the positive and negative aspects of a life are put into a wider context, understanding of who you are and why you are here develops, and much frustration and uncertainty is dissolved.

Negativities   Arrayed around chief feature, and consisting of negative emotions and attitudes, negativities are psychological obstacles that must be overcome in order for the layered self to function at its optimal level and to grow and evolve.

Observation   The practice of using one part of the essence self to observe another part of the layered self in operation to collect observational data. Typically, the intellect is used to observe the emotions in operation. Individuals often use their emotional centre to observe others' behaviour. This can offer useful, even correct, psychological insights. However, the problem with observing via the emotional centre is that judgement, or self-deprecation, or blame, or some other negative attitude often creeps into and colours the observation. To be useful, observations need to be detached and non-judgemental. This is why observing using the intellectual parts of either the intellectual or moving centre is preferred.

Obstacles   In general, human beings do not learn as much when life goes easily and well. Rather, individuals learn best when they come up against obstacles and problems, and when they are confronted by their own limitations and mistakes. Each perceives obstacles and responds to them in different ways. This difference is mostly due to variations in psychological make-up. The life plan is organised so key obstacles arrive at specific stages in their life so life lessons may then be learned. Sometimes these obstacles are so well integrated into daily living that they appear as just another problem to be dealt with. At other times the obstacle arrives from left field and creates a huge disturbance, sending the individual in a new, unanticipated direction.

Orientation   A key trait selected as part of the life plan, it functions collectively with life goal and attitude to shape the essence self's psychological make-up. Orientation provides a psychological means to negotiate tricky life circumstances. When individuals become so caught up in daily life that they lose connection with their spiritual self's drive to learn and grow, orientation steers the individual back onto task. The Michael Teachings identify seven essence level orientations: the pairs of aggression and perseverance, passion and repression, power and caution, and observation.

Psychological mass The everyday identity is constituted of biological drives, essence processes and activities, and socially conditioned attitudes, outlook and behavioural coping mechanisms. These combine to create a psychological mass that causes individuals to move at a particular momentum through life, fending off others by denying, justifying, deflecting or attacking while self-calming in preferred ways in order to maintain its momentum. Inner development requires that this psychological mass be identified, analysed and broken down. Self-enquiry provides the means for achieving this.

Scientific method An experimentally-oriented process used to obtain new knowledge about what happens in the world. When applied to spiritual practices, it facilitates the acquisition of new knowledge empirically, extracting experiential data from personal experience and verifying it the essence self.

Secondary disposition Each spirit possesses a three-fold nature of core disposition, modality and secondary disposition. Secondary disposition influences the way core disposition manifests. It consists of one of servant, artisan, warrior, scholar, sage, priest or king. In the human realm, secondary disposition manifests more directly when interacting with others and primary core disposition remains hidden. The result is that if an individual has a core disposition of warrior and a secondary disposition of sage, others are more likely to observe the sage performative characteristics than the deeper warrior drives.

Self-calming   Self-calming generally follows a shock of some kind in which fear or similar intense emotions are stirred up. It is a psychological mechanism that helps an upset identity return to its accustomed inward state. Self-calming behaviour varies, depending on psychological make-up, but may include eating, drinking, smoking, exercise, playing, shopping, becoming angry, becoming violent, or walking away. All cover over and repress the intense inner response that triggered the need to self-calm in the first place. Self-calming must be overcome to pursue self-enquiry.

Self-defensiveness   Behaviours the everyday identity uses to cope with emotionally upsetting, confronting or invasive life situations. Defensive behaviours are driven by fear and manifest in denying, justifying, deflecting and attacking. An individual's pattern of defensive behaviours are shaped during childhood and teen years. They become crystallised by the onset of adulthood, if not earlier, are embedded in false personality, and then provide automatic responses to threatening stimuli.

Self-enquiry   The process of observing one's inner make-up, analysing psychological processes, identifying positive, negative and self-limiting attitudes, behaviours and characteristics, and working on them to foster personal development.

Socialised self   Is a psychological and behavioural layer within the five-layered self that is shaped by the social conditions into which an individual is born. Language, family, education, social norms, work, opportunities, and so on, all contribute to the formation of the socialised self. As such, the socialised self is a social construct. Self-image is largely a function of the socialised self, being formed as by outside affirmation, repression and neglect, as by inner psychological momentums.

Spiritual self   The consciousness within the five-layered self. The embodied individual's spiritual self is itself a fragment of the individual's larger spiritual identity. The spiritual self's intent is to evolve. It evolves as it embraces a wide range of experiences and learns from them. The spiritual self's goal is to become a loving, knowing and wise identity.

Sub-personality In each life a spiritual identity enters a body and takes on the genetically generated and psychologically conditioned characteristics that together form a unique human sub-personality, or sub-identity. This sub-personality exists for the duration of that lifetime, providing a spiritual identity with the opportunity to explore pre-selected situations and experiences. At the end of the life all the sub-personality's experiences, feelings, thoughts and choices, along with their consequences, are uploaded to the ongoing spiritual individual's accumulated human identity. This provides data that is processed and later used when deciding on future incarnations and other sub-personalities.

Trajectory Each individual has through own unique trajectory through their sequence of approximately one thousand human incarnations. This trajectory progresses through the four developmental levels of infant, child, teenager and adult, with different kinds of choices being made during each phase. This choices made may also be characterised as involving the field mouse, grasshopper, feline and elephant phases. The field mouse is tentative and uncertain, and equates to the infant level of development. During the child and early teen levels, individuals jump more randomly from experience to experience, like a grasshopper. During late teen and much of adult level development individual's make more considered and deliberate choices, like a hunting cat. Choices made during the final part of adult development echoes the elephant, which remembers and moves slowly but with purpose.

True personality Those positive traits present in the essence self that have been selected to implement the life plan. It incorporates skills, abilities and talents, selected from the accumulated human identity, that the individual seeks to develop in this life, along with the positive poles of life goal, orientation and attitude. True personality's qualities are finessed by rubbing them up against the false personality's negative and self-limiting qualities. The process of facing up to these negative and limiting qualities, and overcoming them, helps the true personality learn and grow.

Turning point   A turning point disrupts a life's momentum and turns it in a new direction. Usually such a disruption is key to the realisation of the life plan and involves shifting a life's primary momentum from the everyday self to the essence self. For most people, turning points involve confrontation. External confrontation occurs when one becomes profoundly unhappy with life circumstances, occupation, relationships, marriage, etc. Internal confrontation involves individuals becoming profoundly unhappy with the way they function psychologically, or with how they are living their life. Whether the confrontation is external or internal, individuals reach a key moment of decision, in which they are confronted with their own inadequacies, unhappiness and pain. Often the impulse to confront whatever is inadequate emanates from the spiritual self and is experienced as a series of inner cues.

Understanding   Understanding is achieved as a result of processing the knowledge extracted from life lessons. Because life lessons involve confronting one's limitations and fears, knowledge and understanding are always hard won. The understanding individuals extract from their experiences during the course of their life occurs at the level of the essence self. More usually, understanding is extracted by the spiritual self after a life is over and during the post-life review.

War of momentums The task of becoming spiritual may be described as involving a war of momentums that plays out in the circumstances of your life. It is not an external war between you and others. The war is internal, between the momentum of what the essence self is striving to achieve by putting its life plan into action, and the momentum of the crystallised socialised identity, driven as it is by fears and defensive behaviours that, effectively, prevent the life goal from being achieved. Each life necessarily involves periods during which one momentum dominates, then the other. However, as an identity matures it is better able to sustain its awareness within the momentum of the essence self and so is less disorientated by the opposing momentum of the socialised self. This maturing process occurs both within each individual life and across the trajectory of all lives.

www.ingramcontent.com/pod-product-compliance
Lightning Source LLC
LaVergne TN
LVHW040239240225
804391LV00021B/147